Emily F. D. Osborn

Political and social Letters of a Lady of the eighteenth Century

Emily F. D. Osborn

Political and social Letters of a Lady of the eighteenth Century

ISBN/EAN: 9783337138059

Printed in Europe, USA, Canada, Australia, Japan

Cover: Foto ©ninafisch / pixelio.de

More available books at **www.hansebooks.com**

RIGAUD.

The Honb.le M.rs Osborn
Daughter of Viscount Torrington
and Wife to John Osborn Esq.

POLITICAL AND SOCIAL LETTERS

OF A

LADY OF THE EIGHTEENTH CENTURY

1721–1771

EDITED BY

EMILY F. D. OSBORN

WITH FOUR ILLUSTRATIONS

NEW YORK
DODD MEAD & COMPANY
1891

CONTENTS.

—o—

ILLUSTRATIONS.

—o—

THE SOUTH-EAST VIEW OF CHICKSAND-PRIORY, IN THE COUNTY OF BEDFORD

THIS Priory was founded in the Reign of K: H: II by Rosia, Wife of Paganus de Beauchamp, Baron of Bedford, for Nuns of the Order of St Gilbert of Sempringham; & dedicated to the Blessed Virgin. This Paganus & his Wife gave divers Lands & Priviledges to this House, which were confirm'd by K: E:II. who in the 10 Year of his Reign granted Licence to John Blundel to settle ye Manor of Chicksand & all its Apurtenances on this Convent. —————— The present Owner is Sr Danvers Osborn Bar.t

INTRODUCTION.

—o—

So many records of the eighteenth century have been handed down to us, and are still issuing from the press, in one form or another, that I feel great diffidence in bringing the present collection of letters before the public. But perhaps, as the production of a lady of conspicuous ability and "vigour of mind," as she has been described by one of her descendants, and embracing an important period of history and politics, they may be found worthy of perusal, and may throw some additional light upon the manners and customs of that day.

Also, Mrs. Osborn's relationship to the unfortunate Admiral Byng necessarily involves the introduction of that sad event in her life ; and though his story is a familiar one to all readers of history, it never grows stale by repetition, and an additional interest will be given to the subject by the insertion of some letters connected with it, which have never before been published.

Mrs. Osborn, who was by marriage a great-niece of the now well-known Dorothy Osborne, was a woman of unusual capacity and energy, and the exceptional circumstances of her life were calculated to develop her powers to the uttermost.

She was left a widow at the early age of twenty-four,

and had to undertake the management of affairs in the first instance for her son, then for her grandson, and this she did so effectually that another descendant of hers alludes to her as "one of whom every Byng is proud."

It is necessary, first of all, to give some account of Mrs. Osborn's family history.

Sarah Byng was the only surviving daughter of Admiral Sir George Byng, who in 1721 was created Viscount Torrington in recognition of his valuable services as a naval officer of great distinction. Her mother was Margaret, daughter of Mr. Master, of East Langdon, in Kent. She must have been an extremely pretty woman, to judge by the picture of her which is at Chicksands Priory. Sarah always mentions her with great affection, and after Lord Torrington's death in 1733 they lived much together till she died in 1756 at the age of eighty-seven.

Lord and Lady Torrington had a family of fifteen children, but of this number only six lived beyond infancy, of whom Sarah was the eldest.

She was born in October 1693, at Southill, Beds, just after her father had bought that property, which remained in his family for about a hundred years. Before this the Byngs had lived at Wrotham, in Kent, for many generations.

Lord Torrington's five sons were—

Pattee, born 1699, served in the navy under his father, and married, 1724, Lady Charlotte Montagu, daughter of Charles, Duke of Manchester. Pattee succeeded as second Viscount, and died in 1746, leaving no children.

George, third Viscount, was in the army, married Miss Daniell, and died in 1750, leaving two sons.

Robert, the third brother, was the one to whom all Sarah's earlier letters were addressed, and was evidently the adviser of his sister during her son's minority. He married Miss Forward, was appointed Governor of Barbadoes, and died there in 1740. The present Earls of Strafford are descended from one of his three sons.

John, the Admiral, alluded to as " Jack " in the following letters, was the fourth son. He was unmarried at the time of his death.

Edward (" Ned ") was also in the army, married, 1730, Miss Bramston, of Chigwell, Essex, and died in 1756.

To return to Sarah.

She was not quite seventeen years old when she married, in August 1710, Mr. John Osborn, eldest son of Sir John Osborn, second Baronet of Chicksands Priory. A distance of only three miles or so separated the two houses.

Mr. Osborn's mother, Miss Elizabeth Strode, had died at his birth, and Sir John had married secondly Miss Martha Kelynge, and numerous younger children were growing up and filling the old Priory to overflowing.

Perhaps this may account for a very stormy correspondence which passed between Sir John Osborn and Sir George Byng about this period, as to which of the two fathers ought to offer a home to the young married couple.

I must confess that Sir John Osborn was decidedly the aggressor, and, in his eagerness to throw the responsibility on his neighbour, took little pains to moderate his indignation, and reproached Sir George with meanness in making a demand for £100 yearly, in payment of board and lodging for his daughter and her husband. Sir George, whose replies were of a much more temperate description, concluded by saying that if any more letters were to pass between them, he hoped they should treat each other like gentlemen.

They evidently settled their differences amicably before long, for they were writing to each other most affectionately a few months later, and Sir George was exerting all his influence to give a start in life to Sir John's younger sons. Unfortunately this dispute between the heads of the two families is the only document remaining connected with Sarah's short married life, although we gather that she and her husband lived chiefly with her parents.

In the month of January 1719, Mr. John Osborn died of consumption at Hawnes Grange, near Chicksands, in the thirty-sixth year of his age, leaving her, at twenty-four years old, with two boys — Danvers, born in November 1715, and John, born in 1718. There had been three other children, who had all died in infancy, and were buried in Campton Church, Beds.

The youngest boy, John, died six months after his father, of measles.

Mr. John Osborn's affairs were in a very unsatisfactory state at the time of his death, and his widow bound herself down to pay off the greater part of his debts, for her father-in-law was then an old man, and incapable of transacting business.

Sir John Osborn died early in the year 1720, and Mrs. Osborn then became guardian to her little boy, Sir Danvers, the estates being put into Chancery.

During the sixteen years before her son attained his majority, she took the entire management of the property into her own hands, mastered every necessary business detail, and, with the assistance and advice of her father and of her brother Robert, so successfully wielded the reins of government that she was able to surrender her trust to her son in a greatly improved condition.

Mrs. Osborn's home throughout this period was principally in London, in her house in Conduit Street; but she often paid visits to various friends, and she and Sir Danvers were always welcome guests at Southill. Now and then they stayed at Chicksands for a time; but after Lord Torrington's death, she herself lived more in London.

The next event in Mrs. Osborn's life was the marriage of her son, in September 1740, with Lady Mary Montagu, fourth daughter of George Dunk, second Earl of Halifax.

To his mother Sir Danvers entrusted the task of drawing up an estimate of the future probable expenses of his household, and this she carried out conscientiously, according to her own words, "on a basis of great economy and excellent management." The wages allowed for servants in those days contrast strangely with those of the present day: the butler had £25, footman, £14, and lady's maid, £10; but one must take into consideration the far greater relative value of money 150 years ago.

After barely three years of married life, Lady Mary Osborn died at the age of thirty, at the birth of her second son, John. The eldest son, George, was born in 1742.

Sir Danvers never seems to have recovered his spirits after his wife's death. For some years he led a restless and wandering life, spent some of his time at Horton, in Northamptonshire, with his brother-in-law (the third and last Lord Halifax), and was elected member for the county of Bedford in 1742. In 1745, during the rebellion of the Young Pretender, he raised a troop of men, and led them in person to support King George. In 1750 he went to Nova Scotia for six months on a visit to the Governor, Lord Cornwallis, and three years later was appointed Governor of New York, in succession to Lancy, and sailed from Portsmouth on the 22nd of August to assume his new office. His little boys, meanwhile, were left under the care of their grandmother.

Sir Danvers arrived at New York on October 6th, and died there six days later, but the cause of his untimely death I have never been able to discover.

Once more did Sarah find herself in a responsible position, and once more did she courageously rouse herself to undertake the fresh and unexpected duty which fell to her lot. She was now sixty years of age, and might reasonably have looked forward to repose and peace for the remainder of her days. But her labours were not yet ended.

For the space of another ten years she had to devote herself to the care and education of her young grandsons, and to the management of business during Sir George's minority; and this time she had an efficient coadjutor in the boys' uncle and guardian, Lord Halifax, who, later on, exerted all his influence to start them in their respective professions.

But long before her charges were of an age to be out in the world, the culminating misfortune of Admiral Byng's trial and execution took place, some account of which is given elsewhere in this volume. At the time that this calamitous event occurred, Sarah and her ill-fated brother were the only two remaining members of her family. Her brothers Pattee, George, and Robert had all died some years ago. Lady Torrington died in 1756; and the youngest son, Edward, died towards the 'end of the same year, from grief at seeing his brother John brought prisoner to Portsmouth.

Consequently, Mrs. Osborn, as his only near relation, took a prominent part in pleading for a commutation of his sentence, and, though her efforts were vain, she must have derived some comfort from his dying testimony that she had done all that was possible on his behalf.

There are none of Mrs. Osborn's letters in existence between the years 1751 and 1766. After this date they were, with few exceptions, addressed to her youngest grandson.

After leaving Westminster School, both boys went to Oxford, but at the age of seventeen George received a commission in the army, and was soon after appointed aide-de-camp to his uncle, Lord Halifax, then Lord Lieutenant of Ireland.

John entered the diplomatic service, held a post under Lord Halifax when Secretary of State, was afterwards sent to various foreign Embassies, and finally became Minister at Dresden in 1771. He died at Rudolstadt, in Saxony, in 1814, "on the eve of returning to England after eight years' detention in the territorys of Bonaparte"—as is recorded on his monument.

Mrs. Osborn's letters were addressed to him to different places on the Continent, though he frequently paid visits to England; and while his brother was with his regiment in America during the War of Independence, John lived at Chicksands, and superintended his brother's estate.

Mrs. Osborn lived to the age of eighty-two, and, before she died, had the satisfaction of welcoming the birth of a great-grandson, afterwards Sir John Osborn.

In conclusion, I beg to offer grateful thanks to the

Duke of Bedford and to Lord Strafford, for the help they have afforded me, and for the loan of documents and letters. The original of twenty-one of the latter are at Wrotham. The remainder are in the possession of my father, Sir George Osborn.

I have every now and then omitted portions relating only to family affairs, and paragraphs that repeat themselves, and have endeavoured as much as possible to retain that which I hope may be of interest to the general public.

The original spelling has been adhered to throughout, and I do not anticipate any difficulty in deciphering it.

EMILY F. D. OSBORN.

CHICKSANDS PRIORY, *June* 1890.

1 7 1 9.

———o———

[THE first document, according to date, in Mrs. Osborn's handwriting, is the following statement of her affairs at the time of her husband's death, including also a copy of his will. The Mr. Peter Osborn referred to is the half-brother of her late husband.]

By an order drawn up by Mr. Townsend . . is to pay to Mr. Peter Osborn £400 a year for keeping Sir John Osborn in Cloaths, house, servants, horses, and in short, everything (his sickness excepted) that shall be wanted at Chicksands, and he gives him direction to pay me fourscore pound a year for keeping my children, their being no provision for them till theire grandfather dies . . . the Gardens we have lett to a man for £30 a year, and he is to find everything without more expence to us.

Mr. Osborn has debts of all kinds out against him, executions and all sorts of bonds and ingagements, but Mr. Townsend is off opinion that as he was not possessed of anything when he dyed, that neither his Father nor Heires can be oblidged to pay anything, but his Creditors seem to have other hopes . . .

15

I have took an Inventory of all his goods, and
lockt them up at Chicksands for nobody as yet
has attempted to seize them.   His horses I could
not keep, so by Mr. Townsend's advice, I gave
notice to the Under Shreive (who had three
executions lodgd against him) that Sir John had
let all his grounds round here, and the Horses
would go stray, so upon that he sent for them,
the Landlord of his Chambers in the Temple has
seized there, but I first had an inventory of all
there, for that will be required of me to do, for if
they ever do give us trouble, as to be sure they
will (for everybody will not lose contentedly) I
shall be brought to a strict oath for everything
that did belong to him.   I have myself engaged
at several times for about £500.   Law cannot
oblidge me to pay it, but as most of it is to
Relations and ffriends, I think myself oblidged
to pay it as soon as posible, I have engaged my
honour and that was all they could tye me by,
therefore I shall save every penny I can to pay it
as soon as posible, but fear I shall not compass it
under two year, for all of it is at present upon
Intrest, which I have hithertoo exactly paid . . .

When I found Mr. Osborn ill, by Mr. Townshend's advice I had a Will drawn by him, which
I hoped to prevail with him to signe, but could
not, however he gave Noris the same will which
I had given him, write out in his own hand, but
neither signed nor dated, nor the names writ

plain, and bid him give it me after he was dead, and tell me it was his Will . . . it is as ffollows—
" This is the last Will and Testament of me, John Osborn of Chicksands in the County of Bedford. I give unto my loving Wife Mrs. Sarah Osborn all my Jewels, plate, and Watches, and all other ornaments she has usaly worn and the sum of one hundred pounds for mourning, all the rest and residue of my personal Estate of what nature or kind soever I give and devise to my said Wife and unto her father the Honble. G. Byng, Kt. and Baronet upon trust, out of the same to raise and pay all such sums of money as I shall justly owe unto any person or persons whatsoever . . . And pay the sum of five thousand pounds unto my youngest son John . . . I give and devise the residue and remainder of my said goods and chattles and personal Estate unto my eldest son Danvers, his Executors and Administrators, in witness whereof I the said John Osborn have to this my last Will and Testament set my hand and seal this day of September, Anno Domini one thousand seven hundred and eighteen."

LETTER I.

[The originals of the first seventeen letters, also Nos. 19, 20, 22, and 23, are in Lord Strafford's collection at Wrotham, and were kindly lent by him to me to copy. Letters 18 and 21 are among those at Chicksands Priory.

The Strafford letters are all addressed to the Hon. Robert Byng, Sarah's third brother, then Paymaster of the Navy. The first is dated little more than two years after her husband's death, and about eighteen months after that of Sir John Osborn. Sir Danvers was at this time not six years old. Sarah is evidently passing a few weeks at Bristol and Bath with her eldest brother, Pattee Byng, and entering into the amusements going on at both places.]

BRISTOL, *June* 24, 1721.

I must beg the favour of my dear Brother Robin to put these Letters into the post for me. I am very troublesome to you but hope you excuse it, your last Letter gave me great satisfaction to hear about my affairs, for I am so far from them that I am almost out of patience, not to be better satisfyed. I have writ to Sly to pay you some Rent. I believe it will be about £36 . . . We have been to see Mr. Southwell's house which is within 5 mile of this place. Vanburg was the Architeck and a clumsy lump of building it is, it cost fifteen or twenty thousand pound without Gardens, and there is no good room in it. Little doors, windows and starecase, a prodigious large house, but all the room taken up in thick walls, and clumsy pillars. The prospect is to the Severn which is very pleasent with the adition of the Ships that are ancord there, the Gardens are nothing neither do I believe they can make any, it is such a stony soile that nothing

can grow, and rocks all about.   Ratclif Church
we have also seen, which I believe is the finest in
England, it is in this City and should be a patron
for all that are built, it was founded by a priest in
Edwd. the 3^{ds} time but newly adorned in Queen
Anns, which I cannot but say is extream fine, but
I am not fond of Churches in that manner.   The
Altar is adorned with painting Guilding and Carv-
ing that it comes so near a popish Church that
my Brother said he could not but fancy himself
abroad.   Besides these Churches they have several
fine buildings as Marchants Hall, the Custome
House, which we have not seen yett.

Thursday we had a Ball, the gentlemen Bor-
rowd the Long Room at the Custome House, nine
cuple, and as the gentlemen Baloted for their
partners they did not all suit well, but as follows :

Mr. Byng.
Lady Tereasa frogmorton, Duke Powis daughter.

Mr. Paulet
Mrs. Bloomer a parson's wife, young, pretty and
        silly.

Sir Robt frogmorton
Mrs. Player

Major Dean
L^{dy} Jenkingson, a very agreable lady, y^r Bro :
        says like Dutches Termoti

Captain Rowley
Mrs. ffleming, a very agreable lady.

Mr. Jennings

Mrs. Jenkingsson

Lieut. of Capt. Rowley's ship, the worst there, wch fell to my lott.

Capt. Wilson

Mrs. Craythorn, y^r Brothers partner in the last ball.

Mr. Parsons

Mrs. Snow

Thus I have given you a discription of our De-vertions here but Munday sennight I find my father comes, and then we shall grow grave, at present we amuse our Selves much. This is all the Account I can give you at present, and must conclude, dear Robin,

> your affect. Sister and
>> oblidged humble Servant,
>>> S. Osborn.

Letter II.

BATH, 30 *August* 1721.

I thank my dear Brother Robin for all the trouble I have given you, and since my necklace cannot be found, I must be contented and am concerned I have given you so much trouble to please my Vanity. . . . You will be surprised at my father coming to town so soon, but an express came down from Sir George Saunders for him, upon Lech—(mere ?) being made a Lord wch was

contrary to all promises made to him that any
should be so till his patent had passed.   He will
be in town a fryday, he went in by Coach this
morning.   Now I must tell you the devertion of
this place.   Last Thursday we came here, that
night a play bespoke by Lady Harold, so we did
not see anybody, next day a ball where we was,
and saw all ye great Ladys.   My Brother Byng
dansed french danses with Mrs. Key, who has
seven thousand a year settled on her, and Country
Danses wth Lady Jemima Grey, Duke Kent's
daughter, we left them dancing and went with
some Ladys to Lindseys where I sate down to
Ginea Comerce with Dutches of Wharton, Lady
Harold, Mrs. Sims (Ld Morton's daughter) Mr.
Cook (Vice Chamberlains Brother) Genl Stanwix
lady, Mrs. Bradshaw, Lady Lucy, myself, etc.,
the pooll seven gineas and I very near wining
of it.

Saturday was a play bespoak by Lady Bristol.
She asked us to go, as we accordingly did, but
first went to make a visit with my father to Lady
ffranklin, in the meantime came to see me the
Dutches of Wharton, Lady Bristol, Lady Lucy
and more of our Ladys, which was a perticuler
favour, they not being of my acquaintance before,
and what is very seldom done in these places.
Sunday to Church and to return all my Visits, then
in to Harison's room, where was a varst number
of people, but I, being not well, came home by

8 and went to bed.   Next day forced myself out
not being willing to indulge, met all our great
Ladys at Lindseys and was visited by L^{dy}
Harold, Mrs. Car and Mrs. Andrewes, but so ill
I was forced to come home early with a violent
cold, and was in a fever all night, and yesterday
much worse with sore throat and pain in my side
that I was forced to be Blooded, and am to-day
much better.   Thus I have told you how we
have spent each day here like a real gosip, but
as I believe you are pretty well dull in town,
I am willing to devert you the best I can.   My
Brothers cloaths are extream handsom and ffit
him exact.   He has been at two balls in his
padesway, so I think he cuts a fine figure here.
Here is Lady Inchqueen and 2 of Ld Essex
sisters, but I am not acquainted with them.
Dutches of Queensborough comes to-night.   My
head akes so much that I hope you will excuse
this my scroll, and I must end.

your affect. Sister
and humble Servt,
S. OSBORN.

Gray ye poet lodges in our house so he has
supt with us.

LETTER III.

[Mrs. Osborn is evidently referring in this letter to
inoculation, which was introduced into England in 1718,
and was violently opposed by great numbers of people.

The three Princesses mentioned are the granddaughters of George I. "Jack" is her brother, afterwards Admiral Byng.]

CONDUIT STREET, *June* 2, 1722.

I was much oblidged to dear brother Robin for your patience in writting down perscriptions for my son, as well as to Dr. Askenhurst for his advice, but he has been too ill for me to venture anything but jist what they have orderd him. Sir Hans Slone and Amions have had him under their care, his swelling under his arm is still open, that is the wound that was made there by it being lanced, it is now held open by a pea. . . . I would ten thousand times sooner send them into a room to catch the smallpox, than poyson their blood in this manner, since there is no knowing when the accidents will end that comes by this pernicious practice.

Munday last was a great Court at St. James's, and most people very fine, but I believe the gentlemen will ware petty-cotes very soon, for many of their Coats were like our Mantuas. Ld Essex had a silver tissue Coat, and pink colour lutestring wascote, and several had pink colour and pale blue padeswoy Coats, which lookd prodigiously effeminate. The three young Princesses dansed, which is a signe they got over their inoculating very well, for I am sure my son could as soon fly as danse. Brother George lives altogether in the Camp, I hardly ever see him.

Bro : Byng is better since he was at Southill, and all are well there but my father. Jack, I think, knows when he is well off, for he has taken up his rest at Danbury.

I doubt not but you had some merry doings at Bristol last Munday, and hope you had a share in the devertion. I can send you no news from this place but what is in the public prints, for I have no men belong to me, so of course can have no news that is authentick.

I believe the country will soon be pleasent, but hitherto I fancy you have had much Rain, for certainly it has been so here, and I remember last year at Bristol it was the same. It spoyls my walks sometimes, for most mornings, instead of ordering my Coach and six, I order my shoes and ten toes to trot away to Chealsey. Your Aunts and all here are much your Servants, but none more so than

your affec. Sister

and humble Servt,

S. OSBORN.

LETTER IV.

August 4, 1722.

Dear Brother Robin will think I am continualy troubling you with letters, but having writ to Mr. Theed before and had no answer, I am willing he should have this carry'd to him, so should be oblidged to you to send one of your porters with it. If he is not at his Chambers, they may leave it with his Clerk, and I should be infinitly oblidged to you if you have any time when you go to the other end of the town, if you would call on him yourself and help solicit for me. The case is this that I have had answers to my Chancery bills, but they proving rogueish ones, and not to the purpose, I am oblidged to file a bill of exceptions to them, and oblidge them to answer more fully. Mr. Theed was to have drawn up this bill before I left town, but it is not yet done, and it should be very soon filld, or else I shall not give them time to answer it in Michaelmas term, and I am quite weary of so many delays. . . . When they see a man appear for one they will not delay so, but a poor woman is made nothing off, she may live upon air seven year if she can.

I hope you had my letter of joy to you, but I supose you have so much bussiness now that I must not expect to hear from you.

Brother Byng talks of going to town next Tuesday or Wednesday to see the Duke of Marlborough's funeral, which they say will be extream fine.

All here much your humble Serv^{ts}, but none more than

your affect. Sister

and humble Servant,

S. OSBORN.

LETTER V.

[The Mr. Layer alluded to in this letter was a barrister, who was accused of conspiracy against the king, found guilty, and hanged.]

DANBURY, *Nov.* 30, 1722.

I was in hopes before this to have heard from dear brother Robin, but will supose you have been much taken up with more weighty affairs at your Office, and also hearing Mr. Layers trial, and such things of consequence, but should have took it for a favour to have been in your thoughts Wednesday.   All here rememberd your health, and joynd with me wishing your years may continue to prosper with as much success as they had hitherto done.   I wanted much to see you after I had talked to the lawyers, before I came out of town, but not being able to get them togeather till the night before, it was imposible to see you. . . .   I must beg you will be so good to take my Affairs under your management.   It is a great deal of trouble, and I know not how to ask it, but if you are so oblidging to do it, it will be esteemed a very great friendship and obligation in you.

Haris is slow and delatory in his way, and Theed is so in his.   They both blame each other, and I could never judg between them, but by carrying Haris somtimes to Theed with me, and hear them talk it over before me.   The way to

make yourself master of the affair is I believe
necessary you should read over my bills and
answers in Chancery, which Haris holds and will
give you to read.   The answers I had last sumer
from Messrs. Leigh were not thought sufficient,
and therefore I filed exceptions to them, which it
seems now they designe to argue before a Master
in Chancery.   I should be oblidged to you to go
to Theed, and know when they are to be argued,
and if it would not be too much trouble, I should
be glad you would be in Court when they are
argued. . . .   The Rent is all paid into Chancery,
but we might get an order to permit it to be
put out on India Bonds, etc., that I might have
Intrest, and not let it lye dead—for their is
above £600 paid in there wch lyes dead without
interest.   There has lately been a supena served
upon Sr Danvers and another for myself to fore-
close the equity of redemption of the mortgage.
. . . You must have a full account of their proceedings, and not shuffle you off as they do me,
by saying they will take care and do all that is
proper.   They are all Rogues, but I cannot but
say Theed has dealt as honestly by me as any
one of them, and shuffled less, but he is very
faulty in delaying geting the perticulers drawn of
Newgate Market Estate, wch you must press him
for, for until they are drawn no one can see the
value of it in order to buy it, and it is a great
determint to Sr Danvers not to have that Estate

sold because he is oblidged to pay Intrest for money which should be paid off by the sale of that Estate. . . . To ffollow this will tyer you to death. . . . I shall be satisfyed in general to know you undertake to be my Solicitor. . . . I hope it may lye one day or other in my son's power to be able to serve you or yours and acknowledge the favour you do his mother, for our good Book says there is great merit in assisting the fatherless and Widow, and to see them that are in need and necessity have right, and I am sure I must claim y^r friendship under all these titles.

I will trouble you with no more now, but conclude with the adition of subscribing myself

your most affect. Sister

and humble Servt.

S. OSBORN.

LETTER VI.

DANBURY PLACE, *Decr.* 19, 1722.

I am much oblidged to dear Brother Robin for the account I received from you by Sunday post of my affaires. I am perfectly easy and satisfyed they will be well managed now you have undertook the trouble . . . next time I must desire you to ask Haris for all the papers concerning the poor at Chicksands, for I very much want them.

Last week I was at Purleigh and Screens,

played at cards there till 2 in the morning. But London hours very ill suite the country.

We have read your new play, which I doubt not but you have seen more than once, but we cannot relish it here, and therefore conclude tis our want of tast, since the Beau Mond are of a diferent opinion. Mr. Bob ffytch comes home a Saterday. He has been very ill of a feavour, and has not yet quite recovered it.

your affect. Sister and
oblidged humble Servt,

S. OSBORN.

My love to Nedy.

LETTER VII.

DANBURY, December 28th, 1722.

I received dear B^r Robins by Sunday post, as also one from Haris. . . . He says I must come to town to be admitted in Court as my son's Guardian, to answer the Bill that is preferd against him. If it must be so, I hope it will be so contrived that I may stay but one day in town, for I have not half a crown of my own in the world, and therefore can bear no expence but that which is unavoidable. You are very good to call on my tedious people. Once being spoken too by a man has the weight of ten times a woman's speaking. Mr. Theed must be hurryd out of his life to get Newgate Market sold. That would

greatly ad to the peace of all, for tis a torment to
have that so long about.

I am y^r aff^{te} Sister

and humble Servant,

S. Osborn.

A happy Xmas and many happy New Year to
you.

LETTER VIII.

Munday, March 11, 1723.

Dear Brother Robin is very oblidging to assist
me in so often seeing my Lawyers, which doubtless
hastens them, notwithstanding it seems to move
slowly on, nobody that has not experience of the
delays of that proffession can imagine the plague
of them. I know there is people think it more
my fault that this afaire is not sooner concluded,
but I have bought my experience dear. I know
tis their Ignorance makes them say so, therefore I
mind them not. . . . I beg the favour you will
settle about the security. If the Chancery would
allow it, and the other side agree, I should think
India Bonds or Navy Bills, for the Land and
Malt Tax carry but 3 per cent. . . . and the
Intrest will hardly answer the charge of puting
the money out. I am very easy Brace should
administer. I have no Will nor anything of Mr.
Osborns, and have signed a renunciation to
Brace.

When the perticulers of Newgate Market is done . . . then there is to be two Citty surveyors to value the houses, and since you are so good to take the trouble upon you, I hope you will go through with it all, and press this affair to be wholy compleated . . . and then I hope among some of your rich Citizens that there will be a purchaser soon found, for the Estates being sold will go a great way in setleing our affaires, at least in what relates to Sir Danvers. He is so young that I hope I shall get all his affaires perfect before he comes of age that he may enjoy it all without the Torment I have known with it. Ask Mr. Theed when he thinks we shall be able to get any witness to set aside the Mortgage, wether he remembers Sparahawk the atorney in the Country that promised to let him into many of Weedon's villinanys in this affair. . . . I would have for my Councill, Mr. Talbot, Sir Phill York, and Serjeant Chesyere, so pray take care that these are not retained on the other side.

I am uneasy to find my Leter so long and only filled with my own troublesome affaires, and nothing to entertain you. I find the town and parliament is in full employment, and hope all things will be brought to light, and those suffer that ought to do so. The Country begins to be very pleasent, and this place is always so, good company, a pleasent park and delightfull prospects,

and everything that contribute to make a Country
life agreable.

I will trouble you with no more now but that I am
y^r affect. Sister and

oblidged humble Servant,

S. OSBORN.

LETTER IX.

DANBURY PLACE, *Sept.* 27, 1723.

DEAR BROTHER, — When ever I set pen to
paper it is always to give you trouble, and
encrease the obligations I have to you. Aunt
Lucy being out of town oblidges me now to do
it by beging the favour of you to pay some bills.
I have enclosed them to my father for you,
hearing there must not be any double Letters
directed to you. I have also writ to my father
to pay you £45. . . .

I can entertain you with nothing from hence,
not being at the Assembly yesterday, but there
was much company. Mrs. ffytch hopes you
will come down to the last, which is Thursday
senight. I am glad to hear Bro : Byng is going
to devert himself at the Bath while the Hurry of
removing is over in Albermarle Street. I am in
great hopes of bringing my Cause to a hearing
this Term, and Mr. Bramston who is my Clerk
in Chancery thinks there is great reason to
believe the Mortgage will not be proved to be
a good one. My money is at last put out on

Bank Anuitys, so by degrees I get but slowly
forward.   I may hope a little time more will
make me easy.   All here are much your Servants, but none with more Truth than

y^r affect. Sis^{tr} and

oblidged humble Servt,

S. OSBORN.

I heartily rejoyce to hear Jacky is a Lieut.
I hope it does not want confirmation.   Let me
know if it is certainly so, or only supposition.

LETTER X.

SOUTHILL, *May* 17, 1726.

I must trouble dear Brother Robin with thanks
for your last Letter, and glad the Yorkshire
money is in your hands; for by a letter from
Mr. Theed, I hear the Dean of York is come to
town, and the Life is now to be renewd imediatly, and I am to pay six hundered and twenty-
three pounds for the new one he grants me.   In
the first place we have a dificulty who he is to
grant it too, Sir Danvers being a minor it cannot
be to him.   I may marry again and therefore tis
not thought proper to grant it to me, and therefore Mr. Theed has desired me to consider of
two people I can trust to have it granted to them.
I have chose your self and Thomy Osborn, and
hope you will give me leave to do so, because it is

C

not safe to have it granted to any but those that are just and honest, so hope you will have no objection . . . it being not to give you any trouble more than to make use of your name, and upon any occasion of surrendering it up to have another Life renewd, it must be done by you.

The next dificulty I am under is to raise the sum of £623, for by my paper enclosed you have but £441 in your hands. I did not imagine this money would be wanted till I had received Newgate Market rents, so that what to do for y⁰ £181 I know not. I have writ to Aunt Lucy to try to borow it upon a pressing ocasion. All the favour I ask of you is to answer the whole sum when it is demanded of Theed. I will take care you shall be repaid in less than a week . . . do not let me loose my credit in not having the payment answerd, for I have orderd Theed to draw upon you for £623 whenever the Dean is ready to sign. Pray let me have two words from you by next post. I am always in that unhappy state to be wanting favours, and never in a Capacity to return them. I hope I shall soon overcome all my dificulty that I may not be such a continual trouble to my friends. If you excuse this you will infinitly oblidge

your most affect. Sister and
oblidged humble Servt,
S. OSBORN.

LETTER XI.

[Pattee Byng had married, in 1724, Lady Charlotte Montagu, which explains why she speaks of Kimbolton as her brother's home.]

SOUTHILL, *July* 12, 1726.

I have not had the pleasure a great while of a line from dear brother Robin, and hope that by this time that part of the money is repaid to you, but I have spent a fortnight at Kimbolton, my brothers home, which hindered me writing or hearing of Bussiness. . . .

My brother Byng and myself spent our time very agreably at Kimbolton, which is the finest house and Park I have ever seen, tho not contented with enjoying that alone, we went to see several other places, Boughton, which is the Duke of Mountagues, and Drayton, Lady Betty Jermains, both in Northamptonshire. The first was a prodigious building and great designes were formed by the late Duke, who only finishd one ffront. The gardens and Wood is certainly fine, but I think wants variety, being all an entire deep shade with fine Lime trees and grass walks. We saw it to much disadvantage, the Bridge being broak that we could not see the Water-works which they say are fine; and indeed the Gardens and House are both ill kept, the Duke not being there above a fortnight in 2 or 3 year, and all the furniture except fine family pictures is taken down for other houses.

Drayton is an old house that pleases me very well, built with Towers, not regular within, but fine Galereys, and a very agreable place if it were not so dull looking.

My Brother and the Duke spent two days abroad without us; went with Sir W^m and Sir Gilbert Pickering to Whitlesey mere a fyshing in a Yatch. The weather proved fine and they came home well pleased with their expedition which seldome happens when it is proposed. It is a Lake in Huntingtonshire, 22 miles round, and the narrowest place over it is 4 mile broad, so that tis a perfect Sea. There is Cuts that run from it down to Lyn, and so into the sea.

Since we came home, which was last Wednesday, have been in a continual hurry. Thursday by invitation dined at the Duke of Kents. Fryday we were dressd and in the Coach to go to L^d ffitzwilliams, but rain prevented us. Saturday we was to wait on our new neighbour, Mrs. Beacher. She was a good fortune tho a Brewer's daughter at Hackney, so you may imagine she is nothing extraordinary, but Mr. Beacher will have money to build a new house, and those are, they say, the chiefe ingredients towards a happy life.

Sunday we was again dressd, but the rain prevented our going to Ampthill. Yesterday

we had the Duke and Dutches of Kent and Mr.
Cole with them, also the Herveys, and this day
are for the third time to dress for Ampthill, and
now I have given you a short account of our
time.   I must only ad the humble Service of all
here to you and ashure you I am,

Dear Brother Robin,
most affect. sister and humble Serv',
S. Osborn.

I should think it impossible for Uncle Byng to
hold a month longer, it is not to be expressed
what he endures, a most melancholy end, poor
man, he makes, and every day one wishes might
be his last.   Saturday nobody expected he could
have outlivd, fell into great passions of tears,
and took leave of his family with recommending
the care of them to my father.   Indeed she has a
miserable time of it, and night and day is nursing
him, nobody in the world can take more care of
a man then she does of him, and one should have
thought nothing but the most sincere affection
could have supported any one to go through
what she does, but hers sure must be compassion.

LETTER XII.

SOUTHILL, Oct. 25, 1726.

DEAR BROTHER,—The post I had the favour of
a Letter from you brought us the agreeable news
of your good fortune in the Lottery (which, tho

a Trifle) yet fear it is not true since you did not confirm it by your letter.   Mrs. Byng who heard the number read told us it was my Brother George who had that good fortune.   I wish George very well, but when I consider it is but one main and tis gone, I rather hope tis your own, and hope soon to have the satisfaction of hearing from you that it is so.

To-day my Brother Byng is going to Bedford when there is to be a very great meeting of all the gentlemen in this County, the Secret History of which is that last week there came the Servant of the Bell Inn at Bedford who went round to all the gentlemen, Dukes and Lords without distinction, with the Duke of Bedford's service and to desire their Company to meet him at ye Bell at Bedford tomorow.   This mesage coming by such a messenger, startled every one, and last week Sir Rowland Alston, Mr. Brown, &c., came to consult my father what was to be done, and what was ye meaning of this mesage, for beside it was also to a Tory Inn, and they heard by the by there was a dessign on ffoot for some Propositions against ye next Elections.   In short every one was under dificultys, so my father, Bro :, and several more of the Whig gentlemen went last Thursday to ye Duke of Kent's to consult on this Grand affair, the Odnes of the Mesenger will not permit the Duke of Kent nor my father to go, but they agreed by all means to have all the others go and muster up all the Whigs togeather in the County, as it is the first meeting he has desired with the gentlemen, and sent without distinction of Party, so it was judgd they should not make any, and it was nessesary they should be prepared if he proposed anybody to set up, that then they should oppose any Tory and name another. Duke of Kent would have had my Brother Byng stand but for several reasons it is declynd. Beacher will not be at the expense, therefore at last it was agreed that Ongley has hardly any principles at least not violent if he is a Tory, and that tis nessesary to court him and bring him over if they can to the Whig Intrest.

My Brother Byng carrys him and Brownsel and Hervey with him in his Coach to Bedford, and then is to carry him to ye Whig Inn, where they will meet Alston, Orlebar, and all the Whigs, who are to propose it to him to be beforehand with anything that can be started by the Duke of Bedford who we hear intends to have Leigh and Monox, who are both good Tories, but what will be the end of all this I know not, but think tis a shame to begin already such treatys for people to spend such a large share of money and health as they must do in three year. Tis a sign Duke Bedford is a gidey hot-headed Creature or he would not delight to study an expensive Election to his neighbours, all this is at present under ye Rose, but tomorow it will be known at Bedford, and I thought you would not dislike to know this affair which is but the begining of greater.

My house is done and it will cost me £75 furnishing and all, and £30 was the first sum, with large allowances might come to £50, and now I have spent pounds must save shillings, and I intend to stay here as long as the family does, tho I believe Lady Charlotte has set fryday fortnight. . . .

I have been thinking if I could not have a little assistance from you. I remember once you did scrape up a little chest of candles for Jacky from the office. I say no more, for if it neither suits conscience nor convenience I do not ask it.

You will wonder how I contrive to fill such a large sheet of paper where I have only left room to ashure you I am, dear Brother,

your most affect. Sister and
oblidged humble Servant,
S. Osborn.

Letter XIII.

[This letter is addressed to Mr. Byng at Compiègne.]

Southill, Oct. 25, 1726.

Dear Brother,—It is very obliging in you to give me the pleasure of seeing your hand, and hearing you were well, which favour I received last post. Pleasure and Business no doubt make

great alteration in spending ones time, and makes
one seem to breath a different air at the same
place. This reflection comes from thinking last
year twas all the former, and perhaps this year all
the latter, or rather a mixture of the two that
makes both agreable. Too much of one would
perhaps do one harm, and too much of business
clouds the understanding. I have had more of it
than many women of my age. I own I now and
then wish myself in your pocket, wishing to know
a little truth. We are so humdrum here that we
know nothing but from newspapers. I dont love
to live quite so ffree from the hurry of the World,
without any gentlemen with us, all have deserted
us this summer. My father has not had time
to be hear yet, tho hopes to slip down next week.
My brother is well pleased at Scarborough.
George has taken pet, and says he wont see
us again this summer, and at present dont know
where he is . . . next week I hear he is
to be for 20 days upon Guard at Windsor.
No news of Jack yet, and for Ned he is devert-
ing himself at Danbury, till the Race time in
Kent. Thus you see how forlorn we are, for my
own part know nothing more than conversing
with ffarmers, improving my knowledge in Turnips
and Wheat land . . . and riding out most evenings.
My mother has an extream pretty pad upon
which she and Mrs. Vincent take turns, for we
cannot very well be equipt with more than two.

The Kents went to the Installation, and have not been down since, they being our best neighbours, we miss them much.

After this account what can you expect from this place, especialy when I consider I am writeing to Paris, and to one who knows more than we do here, and therefore must not venture at any sort of news, and for Ilnature, Love, and Envy, they are subjects the town will be ever full of, tho ever so empty of people, but as I never give in to such idle nonsence, nor believe it would entertain you, I shall only tell you I fancy all is made easy again between Tom and his Lady, and they will not part as people was so malicious to say. Tis very hard every little indiscretion in ffamilies must give so much entertainment to other people.

Lucy has got a knack of writeing fine descriptions since she is become a Traveller, which makes me doubt of all y^t was related last year from Paris, since I find she can give as fine an account of the North, and therefore I shall imagine all that is new and charming to her.

I know not how to direct to you, therefore have took the liberty to enclose it to Mr. Walpole. Pray make my compliments of excuse to him for doing so, and believe me, dear Brother,

your most affectionate Sister,

and very humble Servant,

S. Osborn.

LETTER XIV.

SOUTHILL, *Aug.* 21, 1729.

I take this opertunity to welcome you again into England and am extreamly glad you have had a pleasent tour, as the Ladys say it has been. They are in great delight with it, and have great obligations to you for your care of them. I hope we shall soon see you down here. Pray dont neglect us tho it is not so fine at Versaills, we are now reduced to a small family and hope you will not find any excuse to forget your promise of spending a little time with us. . . . Service to George. . . .

your affect. Sister,

S. OSBORN.

LETTER XV.

[This letter is written just after the marriage of Mr. Edward Byng with Miss Bramston.]

SOUTHILL, *Nov.* 28, 1730.

I am indebted many thanks to dear Brother Robin for the oblidging letters since I came here. Your joy and kind expressions to Brother Ned and me on this occasion have been varstly pleasing to me and to my sister Byng, who expresses great esteem for you—she told me you had pleaded hard for your brother. . . . Tho the newspapers have near doubled my sister Byngs fortune in point of wealth, yet what is wanting to make that up, is fourfold made up in her own value, for she seems of a sweet disposition, and formd to make a man happy, indeed I have no doubt but they will make each other so, for I think he has many virtues and is very good-naturd.

How long we stay here is uncertain. They are endeavouring to find a house fit to buy for them in town, which would be best if it can be found at first, because of furniture fiting to it, and Rent runs away with what would purchase on. Their fortunes will be but moderate, for tho she has £1000 a year, yet there is ten thousand pounds debt which must be paid. I imagine she will soon sell her Estate in Essex to pay off that debt, and all she brings beside she must spend, indeed her house will be his, her coach his, &c., but other-ways he cannot spend more than he did before, if so much, and as it is agreed what remains after the debts are paid is to be settled on her self and childeren, and in failure of them to him for ever, but except that hapens, he never will have power to touch one peny more than the income, therefore this was no great catch without the agreable temper she has brought with it, which, as George wrote Ned word, is a jewel whose lustre will brighten by wearing.

I doubt your Aunt Molly, as you call her, lookd very sowr at the news, as to be sure all the Bram-

stons must do.   Her uncle is intolerably vexd,
but answerd my fathers letter with civility, tho
has wrote a very unpleasant one to her.

I will not run on with more, but to tell you we
all drank your health yesterday being the 27th,
and if the winds would have blowd our thoughts
to you, it would have been to ashure you of our
good wishes and none more of them at heart than,
dear Robert,

your very affect. Sister
and faithfull humble Servt,

S. OSBORN.

So many letters every post to bring joys to us,
that our whole time has been spent in reading and
answering of them.   This is near the thirtyeth or
more I have made this week.

LETTER XVI.

CHILBOLTON, *Oct.* 21, 1731.

Dear Brother Robin is very good to give me
the pleasure of a Letter, which I return my thanks
for, and wish I could say anything from this place
which might make this worth your trouble to read.
I must welcome you to your winter quarters,
where I find you are all gathered togeather, therefore pray disperss my complyments among them
and double them to yourself.

Where is George? I hear nothing of him, nor
where he is.   If he is in good spirits, I am easy.

You that are in the midst of the Beau Mond and think of nothing but fforeign Dukes &c., will not be entertaind with what I can relate from hence, which only consists of the pleasures of the ffeild, when last Munday we were perticulerly well pleased, for by invitation we had Dr. Burton, the Master of Winchester School and his ten young noblemens sons that live with him, for which he has £200 a year for each, and is as a private Governour to them, and they also have the advantage of a publick school at the same time, which surely must be a fine way of educating them. These with 4 other young gentlemen of the school met us in the ffeild a Hunting, they and their attendance and ours made in all 40 people, and after very good sport all came home to dine here. Indeed I have not seen a finer sight than these boys and their master together.

Ld Deerhurst and his 2 Brother Coventrys, Ld Ossulston, Lord Brook, Master Duncomb and Sir Robert Burdet, Master Greville, Master Wallop (Ld Lymingtons son), Master Tryon, also Lord Drumlannich the Duke of Queensberrys son, who is under his peculiar care tho not in the house because he would not exceed his fixd number. Last week we spent 3 or 4 days at Lord Lymingtons which is a fine place, and they very agreable people. My 'Lord was so good to engage some of my perplexd affaires which are in so unhappy a situation that no way can be con-

trived to settle them well, but I hope another
fortnight will release me from thinking more of
them for this year.   I beg the favour you will
give the enclosed to Aunt Lucy, and that you will
believe me with great truth, dear Brother,

your very affec^{te} Sister

and humble Servant,

S. Osborn.

Letter XVII.

[There is a gap of nearly two years between this
letter and the foregoing one.   During the year 1732,
Sarah made a tour of three months in France and
Belgium with her friend, Lady Gage, and the journal
she kept during that time still exists among her papers
at Chicksands Priory.]

London, 26 *July*, 1733.

Dear Brother Robert is very oblidging to let
me partake of your devertions and douleurs in
Kent.   I ffeel your situation, but I think there
is not the less life in it for the dull prospect at
present.   Time and patience cures all evils.   I
have been puzzeling over business to-day I
wanted to do before I leave the town, but find
myself less capable of anything of that sort than
in ye midst of a feavour.   It was ye stewards
account nessesary to be passd, but I am forced
to lay them by, find it imposible to proceed.
What creatures we are to have a little Illness
alter the whole fframe!   I shall be quite malon-

choly to find myself so useless if I do not mend very much in the country.

I go to Lord Shannon's a Munday, I believe for the month of August, but that depends on company they expect there, but would not let me stay longer in town, for which they are very kind, for I rather loose than get strength here, and yet grow ffat. My acquaintance in town have been very good to me, I have not been one day alone, so that I really cannot say I dislike being here. I went with Lady Gage to Ashly this week, and returnd in a chaise. I thought I might venture calling half way at Dutches of Cleveland's, where we refreshd, otherways have not been out of my doors since mother went out of town. There is no sort of chat or news, you are in the gay life, and I hope Kent will answer all your expectations, which will be a very great pleasure, dear Brother,

to your affect. Sister
and humble Servt,
S. Osborn.

Bro: George tyerd of Southill, is going to Hampton Court tomorow, not in waiting, so to his lodging there. He intends for Southill again in 3 weeks.

LETTER XVIII.

[This letter is written just after the death of Sarah's father, Lord Torrington, to whom succeeded her eldest brother, Pattee. Sarah takes up her abode chiefly in London after this event, and apparently writes from town to her son, who is evidently at Chicksands, and though only eighteen years of age, is now busying himself with the affairs of the estate.]

Decr 1733.

MY DEAR DANVERS,—Mr. Ware will be with you by 12 a Clock on Thursday, and by farther enquiry of Him I find he is in much esteem, and therefore hope he will prove a propper person to serve you . . . as to my advertized friend I cannot yet be able to come at his character, only that he was heir to the great sportsman fframpton, who left him £800 . . . as you say, Mr. fframpton will have his choice of ffarms, for ten people where I was the other day was enquiring after him, and vext he advertized, but one day I put them all in an uproar by telling them I had sent after him and seen him. They all beggd if he did not succed in you that I would let them know. . . . You would have laughd to have seen everyones distresses unfolded. One cryd " I have a ffarm has lain on my hands this 2 year of £180, and have not rec^d a shilling," another one of £140, another 2 ffarms, and so on till ten had declared to the same effect. This has convinced me that you have no worse luck than others. They were all so eager after this man, that they could not agree who should have the prefference, . . . and if he does not take y^r ffarm, . . . I shall

D

nevertheless be curious to know who is the lucky or unlucky person who gets him. Mr. Nicolson is a gentleman ffarmer that assists Mr. ffytch with his advice and lives in the neighbourhood, and one to whom we have given a little present of Wine for asisting us sometimes, . . . and therefore a very propper person to give advice what you should do. . . .

Brandy, lemons, knives, a copper pot and Jack goes tomorow. Taylor says muggs, punchbowls, and glasses are to be had at Shefford. There is no occasion to give 2 sorts of wine. I hope the basket I sent a Satterday got safe. Emertons people were like all other, very teazing, and sent you down the wrong colours. . . . To be sure you ought to have an Acc^t of all wheat, butter, pidgeons, and everything how sold, and what proffits, and not he pay ye rent and give you no farther account. . . . I believe before this ffarm he was a very honest man, but this either by temptation or stupidity has very much alterd his conduct. I am quite in a Wood and very ignorant in his ffarming Acc^t, however I shall endeavour to state it all in a regular way, and then you must consider the Accounts before they are passd, and I believe you and I should be shut up some hours together before they can be so. I do assure you I am quite out of my depth, and must have y^r assistance.

I am told if y^r walls are not thorough dry your

paper will be quite spoyld, and if they are dry the
best way is to put the paper to the walls without
any liming, if the walls are only one ruff cote and
not whited, but if they are whited, it will not do
so. . . . This is a good scheme to save expence,
and I am ashured 'tis by much the best way
where there is wall.

I know not if Brother George jokes, therefore
say nothing that I may not be bitt, but he yesterday assured me upon his honour that he had it
from good hands that Brother Robert is appointed
Gouvenor of Barbadoes, which is £1200 a year
paid by yᵉ Govmᵗ here and £3000 by the Island
I wish it may be true, tho sorry we must loose
him. If this is really so we must think if he can
provide some maintenance there for yʳ Uncle
Robert (Osborn), if he can be prevaild upon to
go there. Posibly a new Clymate and a distance
from his odious acquaintance may make him
become a new man. He has sense if he would
make use of it, and I am never without hopes
where there is that ingredient, for at one time or
other in Life it predominates over yᵉ Passions.

I hope you burn or lock up my letters, for I
should be prodigious sorry anyone should know
I pretend to offer my oppinion to you, what is
between ourselves goes for nothing, and you
are so good to take it as purely from affection, but a mother is the last person that
other people will allow the previlidge, and there-

fore whatever she says should dye in your own breast.

LETTER XIX.

April 1734.

All the advice Danvers met with when he was in London was not for his advantage, and fearing he should not be a man soon enough, those ways never fail to have their effect, and whenever he returns, is some time before he can setle again. I have heard ffrom Mr. Charles that he has kept very ill hours ever since he went down, and consequently cannot study next day, but makes him very indolent. Two o'clock in the morning is very improper hours, and therefore I should be much oblidged to you to give half an hour of your time to write a litle good advice to him. You may tell him that you met with a person who came from Cambridge of whome you enquired and that they told you of his bad hours, and therefore that the ill consequences that must produce has made you write to him on that subject, and that you imagine I know nothing of it, and say somthing to encourage him to take Mr. Charles advice, for if he does not find the men of the family have an opinion of him, he will have less and less regard for him (Mr. Charles) every day, which will be very unhappy. I will not keep the news longer, and this hint is enough, and I shall be much oblidged if you will

be so good to write this post if you have time.
They think women and parsons dont know the
world, and that it is manly to keep such hours.

I can only ad that I am,

yr very affect. Sister and humble Servt,

S. OSBORN.

LETTER XX.

[This letter is written to Mr. Robert Byng just after
his marriage with Miss Forward.]

CONDUIT STREET, 27 *April* 1734.

DEAR BROTHER,—After hoping you had a
pleasent journey to Plymouth, and that all things
there appear to your satisfaction, I give myself
the pleasure of conveying my good wishes to you,
and imagining you will be glad to hear how things
go here.   I send you the Acc^t of our County
Election, which came on last Wednesday.   Votes
for Spencer were 1351, Alston 1287, Leigh 1020,
by which you will see Spencer had even a greater
majority than my Brother when he stood, and
that was recond a very great one. . . . The
populace of Bedford are most discontented at
having no opposition for the town, and by this
time it is determind if Sir Roger Burgoine and
Mr. Beacher opposed them, the Election was to
be yesterday, and there was schemes to make
that matter bear, tho' posibly without much hopes
of succeeding, the return being doubtfull.   I am

impatient to hear how it has gone. If they succeed, I shall think it a masterpeice. . . . Now I must tell you the long expected match of Lady Ffany Pierpoint and Phill Meadows was concluded last Tuesday from the Opera. She pretended to be ill and went out, neither servants nor chair of her own could be found at that time, and so in a hack chair she went dirictly to Lady Meadows in Priory Garden, where was Parson, Licence, Husband, and all ready. Next day he and she went out of town to his sister Bulstrodes at Hounslough. She was of age the day before, and has given herself and £20,000 entirely to him. I hope she will be as honourably dealt with in relation to the settlement of her fortune, as some people you have been concernd for.

There is not any news yet come of the arrival of the Prince and Princess[1] of Orange in Hollond. The wind is against leting us know soon. There is no doubt they got there safe, and glad he is, I am sure, to set his foot on his own land again. They talk of the Prince of Orange going to the Rhine, a volunteer only, if that is so he has promised the King and Queen that the Princess Royal shall make them a visit. It is to be in two months, and has been a sugar plumb that has had the desired effect, for everyone concernd in their voyage has had faith to believe it, tho I believe none else can, at least it is very improbable.

[1] Eldest daughter of George II.

It made them all go chearfull, when from thinking
not to see England in years, that they expected
now to return in two months. The king said he
would send his yatchs upon the first notice for
her, and take care she should be back again to
meet him at his return from y⁰ Rhine. There is
orders given to buy horses for her to hunt when
the season comes, they are then to be at Hampton
Court. So all this looks serious, and the Queen
talks of it with great pleasure.

The town is a desart, looks like july. How is
it posible to think it April, it has not been so in
this month in anyones memory.

I am with great truth, dear Brother Robert,
        your very affec⁴ Sister
           and humble Servant,
                S. OSBORN.

LETTER XXI.

[Four years elapse before the next letter of Sarah's
is written. In the year 1736 Sir Danvers attained his
majority. The present letter is full of details of house-
keeping and the cost of living, which it is interesting to
compare with the present day.]

              SAVILE STREET, 1738.

MY DEAR DANVERS,—I have wrote so many
Epistles to you this week, that now I think there
is nothing left to say on your own affaires, and
therefore I have set down to consider what you

desired me to do some time ago. 'Tis a subject quite disagreeable, since I cannot endure to think of your being at any expence with me, only when I think again, it is if I do not come to some calculation you will never esteem my House your own, and I cannot be easy if that is not so, for I must desire you to look upon it entirely in that light, and to come and go and do in it exactly the same as if I was out of it, and be without the least constraint or formality in any one perticuler. You must believe this sincere when you reflect that all the satisfaction I can enjoy centers in yourself, and consequently can never be so happy as when it is in my power to contribute towards your ease,—but to the point.

The first thing I lay down is that for 2 or 3 year to come you will enjoy a single life by being here and there and everywhere, therefore I would put this affair in a method that you should never be at expence here but when you are actualy here, and so always carry your expence with you.

The whole of the affair is this, that when I live by myself I generaly spend in what I call house-keeping, which is only eatables, 30 shillings a week. If company or any unforseen thing happens it encreases according to that, but never is under, so that I recon myself and five Servants at that rate, exclusive of Beer, Coals, Candles, Tea, Coffee, Sugar, Wine, and several other articles which slip in to Housekeeping.

When I live alone I only have a slice of the Servants joynt without any adition whatever, but that cannot be if any one person is with me, and whenever you have been at home it has seldome been under £4 a week, therefore I recon one week with another it will generaly come thereabouts, for I recon you will have two servants here, but have more or less, you will only be at the expence you bring with you.

Now consider in what light you would choose to put it. I am uneasy for fear I may not do it in that wch you approve, and that you will by complysance assent. I beg it may be not so. Be ffree and sincere in your Answer, as I am in my proposal, which is, that the fewer articles and trouble you have the better. And I was thinking the expence of Coals, Candles, Beer, Washing, &c., would be endless to devide, therefore supose all these articles sunk, and insted of them you make the table when you are in town, your own. I fear you will think upon first sight of this, that I am unreasonable, in proposing you should keep me and my five servants when you are here, but upon second thoughts . . . you will conclude I do it in this method that you may never have any reconings but the weekly account, and that only when you are here for any time, and hope you will give me leave to treat you with my own short Commons, when only a few days call you to town, then when the table is your own, you may live better or worse as you like, invite what Company you please, and nothing can make you more Master of this house than the table being your own, with a Housekeeper who will take all the care posible to have it ffrugal to your mind. If you rather choose I should put in yᵉ 30 shillings a week in yᵉ house purse, it will be equal to me, and I will then endeavour to devide the other articles. Why I ad washing to them is that when you are at home, I always wash table linnen and sheets abroad. I hope I have explained it so that you understand. I pay for everything but the dirict housekeeping weekly book, which will come to £4 a week, wᶜʰ is however cheaper than you could be at any scrub lodging, and yᵉ Servants at Board Wages, and from this time I desire it may no more be caled my House but your own.

As soon as the great Shefford wagon drove from this door a Wed. there came the great Winchester wagon with a hogshed of 2 year old Port wine between me and my mother. If it should answer, and they generaly have good wine at Southampton, I will have a larger stock, for Port is all I pretend to, and therefore would if posible have it in perfection. By all means write again to the Duke of Beaufort, and take the liberty to remind him that the years Interest was due the 19th of last month, that you have engaged to pay £300 the 24th of this month, and

depend upon his being so good to order the payment of against that day, and should be oblidged
for answer at Lord Torringtons, Southill, Biggles-
wade, Beds.   I hope Brother George got down
well this terrible day.   I pitty poor Jack and
more ye Chester in ye downs.   The wind is quite
frightfull.

My duty and complyments to all,

your truly affect. Mother,

S. O.

They say Sir Orlando is taken by Mr.
Edwards, one of his creditors, and bringing up to
ye Fleet prison.   Twas madness he did not go
abroad after he was discovered.   There is a
severe criticism on Popes Essay on Man.

LETTER XXII.

December 26, 1738.

DEAR BROTHER,—My head is so full of what
Brother George told me yesterday, that I cannot
help sending you my joy, for tho there is many
disagreeable things in it, yet the main must be
considerd.   He declard to me upon his honour
that he had it from very good authority and
out of Sir Charles Wade's house that you were
appointed Governor of Barbadoes.   If this is so,
why should you deny your ffriends the pleasure
of hearing what must please them, if it does you ?
I dont let it go out of my lips to any one, but he

told it at Stuckley's, and was so serious that we all bile at it. Sister Byng assured me it was no jist, he told us all perticlers, that you have it in a very handsome manner, without any clog upon you. Stuckley in a moment was thinking who to send with you, and I imediatly was thinking how I could serve you here, and take care of your eldest son in your absense. It has so engrossed my thoughts that it spoylt my devotion yesterday.

Pray answer this letter next post, and with my compliments to you all, I am,

y^r very affect. Sister

and humble Servant,

S. O.

LETTER XXIII.

[This is the last letter addressed to Mr. Robert Byng. He died the following year.]

CHICKSANDS, *January* 30, 1739.

DEAR BROTHER,—Many thanks for a cargo of paper come a Thursday. Unreasonable consciences are still asking, if it is not too late for your almanacks, I should be obliged to you for one, and a large ruler, with pencils, a little red Ink, a little Pounce, a piece of tape, for I am much employd at present in what I am distressd for these things, and can get nothing here, not so much as a penknife to scratch. . . . And if any of your clerks are at leisure, could you employ one to rule twenty sheets of the enclosed large paper. . . . I am ashamed of all these troubles we give you. My son . . . is frighted at borrowing money and mortgaging, and therefore is most inclynd to what is a certainty, tho in ye end not so proffitable. You are very oblidging to think so much for him when you have so many material affaires of your own to take up your mind, wh : I hope will prove to your satisfaction and advantage. Be assured in anything Danvers or I can serve you in your absense, that you may depend upon our best care, therefore in all y^r schemes take it for granted we are ready to obey your orders, and shall do it with pleasure, beside the natural affection and regard I must always have for you and yours, you have a strong claim to all our concern from the obligations we have received from you, and which we both gratefully acknowledg. My Brother Torrington came down Sunday, dind here yesterday, goes to London tomorow. He says Henry Osborn goes to Guinea and Jack with you to Barbadoes, and may be worth his while from a good understanding between the Governor and his brother : if that is so, tis very well, otherways methinks you are all agoing from us, but I dare not reflect too much on the disagreable part, therefore will stop on that subject. Can you spare two days when ye coach comes for me ? I desired Lucy to propose it, and do as it suits you. I would

have gone up with Brother Torr. tomorow, but
Danvers desired I would stay a little longer.   He
finds a woman nessesary in a house, which I
hope will inclyne him in due time to think of a
companion for himself.

Lady Ann Lumley I hear is to be married this
week, and Lady Ann Montagu to succeed her as
Lady of the Bedchamber.   Lord Halifax is
lucky to get rid of two daughters so soon.   My
compliments attend Sister Byng and yourself,
dear Bro :

y^r most affec. Sis. and faithfull Servt,

S. O.

Send us a litle parliam^y news if any worth
pening.

LETTER XXIV.

[The next twenty-four letters are all addressed to Sir
Danvers Osborn.   The French Bureau described in this
letter is still at Chicksands Priory.   The Duke of
Manchester here mentioned was the second Duke of
that name, who had married the Duke of Montagu's
daughter.   The Duchess of Marlborough Mrs. Osborn
speaks of, was the widow of John, the hero of Blenheim,
Ramilies, etc.]

SAVILE STREET, *October* 27, 1739.

MY DEAR DANVERS,—I much long to hear from
you that your cold is gone, and as Lord Halifax
comes to-day, and the Ladys next week, I shall
hope to hear you have Dr. Crane with you.   My

heart akes when I think how low spirited you are there by yourself.

The Wind I doubt changd too soon for Brother Robert, it is feard they are blowd into Plymouth. I had a letter from him dated Munday morning at 8 o'clock. They were then going through the Needles, and if the Wind lasted two days, hoped to loose sight of Land, but I fear it changd Tuesday morning.

I have ruind you by buying the very handsome ffrench Bureau. Lord Essex I believe bid against us, and therefore brought it up to twenty guineas, and we bid tother crown, and had it. It is now in my parlour, and I cannot grudg the money since it is an extream handsome one, and you could have had no English Bureau under £16 or £17, but if you do not care for it, I can part with it for what I gave. Tis tortoiseshell inlaid very fine with brass, and wants no sort of repair, it is the same sort of what stands in the two Piers at Lord Carterets. This is very fine and large of the sort. . . .

I hope you had oysters last week? Would you have them once a week or fortnight?

I send you "Common Sense" to shew the spirit designd. One was sure the case would turn out so, where party rage must guide.

Lord Robert Montagu and Dutches Manchester came to town together last Wednesday. She went dirictly to Dutches Marlborough, who had prepard an Apartment to receive her whenever it happend. I saw a Lady yesterday, came piping hot from thence, left the old Dutches at cards, and exercising her Witt on ye poor Duke's will, commends the Dutches who is in high favour at present, she has talkd so sensible and propper on the occasion. She is charmd with her, but the Will is her whole rediculе, and since it is so, tis pitty he named his Dutches in it. He has left her £300 for mourning, which is not 3 pence, her watch and jewels for life, and after to his brother. This is set out by saying ye watch cost I forget what, when she married in her youth. She has broke it and changd it away for one that cost but £14. The baubels of jewels are set in the same light, but the great Joke of all is the Sedan chair, which cost £30 at her weding, and now not worth £4. The furniture of the two rooms which the Dutches of Marlborough had given her was not treated with so much contempt, but calld a "few old goods."

This is the whole left the Dutches, he has left everything in Lord Roberts favour, being sole executor, not a farden to his sisters, not even mourning, which is a litle hard on them. £25,000 in money is ordered to be laid out in Land in Huntingtonshire, and entaild on with the Estate. Half a years wages to all his servants, and nothing left to anybody beside. Dutches Marlborough says he has left his Dutches and all

his Serv^{ts} a half years wages, for £300 was half a
year's pin mony, so she puts it in that light.   It is
no wonder anywhere else but at Marlborough
House that he should do all he could in favour
of his Brother, since there is so small Estate
to support so great a title, and £2000 a year
joynture to be paid out of it to a young woman
may live this fifty year, but at Marlborough
House all is calld mean spirited.   I doubt nothing
would have made it noble but leaving his Dutches
the £25,000 cash.   All else was trash, for she
says she must starve on her joynture.   Some say
all the jewels she had was presents from her own
family, if it was so, tis pitty they were not entirely
given to her, but this will was made at Kimbolton
2 years ago by a country lawyer, who I supose
made all returnable, even the sedan chair, through
Ignorance.   However I well remember how they
treated the Duke of Bedfords character when his
Dutches died, and therefore am not astonished to
hear the same now.

The estate is recond £4000 a year, and the
place in the Customs £1500, out of which L^d
Robert had an anuity of £600.   I dont recon
he will have above £3000 a year adition with his
title.

Undertakers dont go down to Bath till Tuesday,
then they bring him to Slough, and so to Kimbolton, that it will be at least Sunday or Munday
next before he is burried. . . .

I dont see that you might have been his Succeeder in Parliament, for Clerk has not a foot of land in that County, 'tis Dr. Alured Clerk's brother. . . .

I have wrote enough to make your head ake to read.

Dont leave it upon your Harpsichord.

I am your very affect.,

S. O.

Princess Wales to see Dutches Bedford a Wednesday. Child xtiand Thursday. That day and yesterday saw company there. I met a thousand people I did not think had been in London.

LETTER XXV.

From SAVILE STREET, *November* 8, 1739.

MY DEAR DANVERS,—My cold still keeps my spirits so low, that I have not been out three times since you went, and therefore have not that joy you imagine by the town ffilling, which it does now every day.

I have amused myself with clearing away draws full of old letters and papers, to save you the trouble of making a Bonfire of them. I should have reserved them to have amused you, if I could imagine they would ever have been read by you, and only y'self. Many of them have made me vain, but more have extinguished that weakness by bringing maloncholy past sceans into my

remembrance.   Some from my father with such
tenderness and esteme for you that I must still
preserve them for your perusal, and tho it may
be ffashion to explode such tenderness and
humanity as I have lately been reading, yet I
thank God for having been born in the days when
such passions were praiseworthy, and having
received the Benefit of them from my ffriends,
for it surprises me to collect together the heap
of civilitys and kindness I have received, and the
great want I was in of them.   I hope distresses
will lessen as inhumanity prevails, and wo be to
those who are, and are to be born.   My latter
days have been so much happier that I had forgot
how I strugled in Life in my youth, till this leisure
time has refreshd my memory.

The Duke of Manchester was to lye at Baldock
last night in his way to Kimbolton.   He has been
very oblidging to the Dutches, given her the
offer of the house in Grosvenor Square until she
can ffit herself, also the use of what plate she
pleases . . . has carried her £100 for fear she
has no money.   She is sensible of all his civility,
and has behaved exceeding well . . . his own
Dutches removes in his absense to Grosvenor
Square, at least till the lease is out, there being
little trouble to step into that house quite ffur-
nished, and even coals laid in for them.   He has
given his sisters mourning, but that or anything
else will not content them, they are outragious

that their Brother did not leave them it.   Their
affairs will be the Conversation of yᵉ town till some
other person makes a new subject.

I am, my dear Danvers,

your very affec.,

S. O.

I am sorry to hear Ashby is taking the mills
at Langford, for you will loose a good Tenant, . . .
but you know your own affaires best.   A letter
from Jack to-day—still at Spithead waiting for
ships he is to convoy to Haddock, expects daily
to go.   He thinks they (Bro. Robᵗ) are got to the
Madras by this time, and we may hear from them
from there.   I am old fashion, and cannot be easy
till I do. . . .

LETTER XXVI.

[This letter is full of the preparations for the marriage
of Sir Danvers Osborn with Lady Mary Montagu, fourth
daughter of the second Earl of Halifax.   The wedding
took place in September.]

CHICKSANDS, Aug. 26, 1740.

My heart goes pit a pat for fear you will come
before we are in order.   If Tables and Glasses
dont come till Thursday sennight, I hope at least
you wont come before Saterday after, for as that
Thursday will bring so many things, what shall I
do with you to come the same day, and fryday
must not be a weding day, for it is unlucky, there-

fore I shall scheme all for Saterday sennight, for
it is not possible you can come here sooner.   I
wish Pattee or anybody could look at any of the
auctions or places they sell at in Jermyn Street,
and find two old half settees for a trifle, to cover
with the red stuff damask to match the six chairs,
for I dont think the velvet armchairs do so well
there as by the Bedside.   I feel like Martha, carefull and troubled about many things.

Next week the wood holes must be filld, the
evenings grow cool. . . . I have set Lady Mary's
dressing table in foylight (firelight ?) and find it
must be very inconvenient to her not to have a
large glass in the pier where one was before, for she
is too tall to dress her body by the glass upon the
table.   I wish you could meet with any old fashion
pier glass to put there. . . .

I am in a hurry, only time to assure you I am,

y^r affect.,

S. O.

Austin dont in the least care for this Job of
Work, first he don't understand it, and second
he is getting things for the fair, and he says no
men to be had to help him. . . . It will not, I
daresay, be done this two months, y^r Pew alone,
he says, will be a fortnight doing.   Leck must set
up the Glasses when they come, for nobody here
can fasten them to the stoco, or put the whole
lengths in their frames.

LETTER XXVII.

CHICKSANDS, *Sepr.* 7, 1740.

I imagine I shall hear from you tonight, and now expect every Letter to fix the day of your coming.   Pray at least guess about the time, for things must be had or bespoke beforehand.   I have sent to the ffyshman at Eaton.   He was there last Tuesday, says he has no good fysh yet, but will call again Tuesday, and then I must bespeak ffysh for fryday, or whenever I take it into my head you will come.   Then ffryday will bring all relations, as those from Southill and Clifton, and the next ffryday after being a good moon, will bring the neighbourhood, therefore I shall calculate for two ffrydays, and after that you may rest.   The chimdy man is not yet come, . . . it is better but not yet cured, it will do with a coal fire, but wont bear a blasing fagot.   They are all of oppinion that nothing will do but putting it down, . . . but the next chimdy is stone, and if this was brick, you might not like it, and tho there is stone enough to do it, the masons work would come to £5, and the Bricklayer's to £2, and this it must come to at last, and have a funel to itself, it is now so crooked and small tis imposible to have a draught.   Rogers knows it is the only remedy, which makes him so tyersome about it, . . . and I dare not venture to order it without you.

The room is finished, the Glasses prodigious handsome.   I shall kill Bailis if the Tables do not come next Thursday. . . . Whatever marble you are to have is already in England, there is no ffresh blocks coming from Italy.   I am quite pevish with her dilatory proceedings.

If those tables and your presses were come, we should be compleat, except a Hearth and Doggs for the drawing-room.   Shovel and tongs came on Thursday.   What did they send a poker for?   Shovel and tongs for dining-room, antyroom, your Library, and two rooms in ye new pasage cannot be done without there are dogs and hearths sufficient.   I am persuaded you will be pleased with ye furniture of that room, tho it is but paper. . . . The tea kettle is come, and I hope you think it varstly handsome, and I hope it will not exceed what I shall be able to compass, desireing you to accept it as my present to y'self.   Brother Robert has remited me more money, and desires I would let Waples have £500 if he wants it for a purchase.   For Godsake tell Waples he must make no such purchase, for my Brother does not consider what he has sent for, . . . he thinks I put Guineas together that will produce, he recons much too fast.

I have drawn out your supper, send me word if you approve, or alter it as you like.   I have given Mrs. Porter dinners and suppers for a week, for the first week must be all clatter and hurry, and the more so the better. I hope I shall keep well till after that time is over, but I have had a return of my old complaint, has put me much out of spirits. All the poor chicks are fat, and from this time will grow large and lean again, but they must frigacy or do somthing, no Agheraust (?) with Partridge, what shall I do? Three of them and two quails is all we have yet in. The men, Norman and everybody I believe has made Harvest Home. Pryer says he has not had such fine wheat nor so much since he was in the farm. . . .

Dr. Osborn was here in a hurry about the Hoo, says if you dont have it, Mr. Edwards will, and that he wont take less of him than 1800 guineas, his wife dont care he should part with it under. I told him I daresay you would not be his hindrance from getting a good price.

LETTER XXVIII.

SAVILE STREET, *October* 28, 1740.

I am glad the Chapple is done, and succeeds to your mind. The pulpit furniture is done, and goes down tomorrow; it had been with you last week but by a mistake. I brought up the old pulpit cushion to be ffitted to the size and coverd, and when I took off the old rotten cover there was wrote upon the dimoty, " Dorothy Osborn, the year 1605. B. D."

Therefore I preserved that end and cut the other,
since it had been 135 year in your chaple, and I
conclude the old green Cloath has been so too.
I shall be glad if you and Lady Mary like what
is sent; it is done in the cheapest manner it could
to be decent.   There was down enough in the
Cushion to make 2 Cushions for the Books upon
the Communion Table.   I think you will want a
Common Prayer Book for that.   I hope this
Crimson won't offend the Doctor Osborn.   He
was a litle outragious at the Colour.   I unfortunately called it red, and that is not so right for a
Chaple.   Is he reconciled to the Tapistry at the
Altar ?   He is not sure if that does not favour a
popish one.   There goes a Box with your Books
tomorow, and with the chapple furniture, a Box
of flowers for Lady Mary and her Mantelette,
also her two Boxes from Chavenix and a toast
fork for Breakfast; but I beg she may not break
her back with stooping to make toast herself.

Your punch Ladle was broke it seems, and
came to be mended, and goes also tomorow.   I
name these things that you may order them
y'self, for they had got a way of opening everything that came, and twas ten to one if I knew
of it.   I hope they did not serve you so with the
oysters.   The only reason I wished to know if
you had them was if they were good, or if more
would be acceptable to you.

'Are these things so ?' is a very severe Poem;

tis said to be wrote by Dodington. I send you that also tomorow. I have pack up one of the old frames which I gave 6 pence for, it must be gilt over and then will be as handsome as your own. I am getting in all your bills. You have not sent your Seal to be new cut, or said if you had your watch.

My dear Danvers, I am,
most affectionately yours,
S. O.

I will if posible send 6 hasocks tomorow, there are 2 dozen of yᵉ ordinary ones in yᵉ Long Gallery. . . .

LETTER XXIX.

ARGYLE STREET, *June* 16, 1741.

MY DEAR DANVERS,—You need make no excuse for opening my letter, you very well know I have no secrets from you, and as it came from Barbados, I concluded you read them all. However as there is another ship come in today, I will stay for other letters, before you need write about that affair. The man of war which is to bring them was arrived at Barbados, therefore I conclude them now to be upon the Sea, and that they will be home the latter end of July.

Nobody is yet in your house. It is lockd up and yᵉ keys here. John goes there morning and night, that nobody knows but what he is in the house.   What maid are you to have when you come ? for the house must be dusted against you come.   Mary may be y^r maid while you are in town, for in a week or ten days I shall go to Shannons to stay till October.

The secret is concerning the Election.   They are not properly chose, and there must be a new Election, but for godsake dont let a word drop about it.   You are apt to leave your letters in the Library, and I dare not explain more, and even this burn imediatly.

Lady Mary and you are very oblidging to accept of my good intentions, which must always be sincere in serving you and her, for while she loves you I must love her, and really do.   Pray give her my thanks for her kind letter which I intended to answer this post, but have been prevented.

Lord Oxford died this evening at six.   Lord Duplin gone to Ireland, and I think leaves his Lady with his mother in Yorkshire.   A monstrous fortune she is, but with them great fortunes there generally is a But.   The provoking boy has neither brought St. James nor Gazeteer.   I have sent again, and he is gone out with all in the shop.

yr. very affect.,

S. O.

Prince and Princess are at Lord Carteret's to-night. . . .

LETTER XXX.

ARGYLE STREET, *Oct.* 10, 1741.

MY DEAR DANVERS, — I must welcome Lady
Mary and yourself to old Chicksands, where I
dont doubt but you find charms you did not meet
with at finer places. The Old Proverb says
home is home, be it ever so homely. Indeed
I always find it so, and really my Bandbox, for
so I must call it, is very agreeable to me. Indeed
you have made it so by extra ornaments I should
never have thought off. Upon the whole, tho I
am vexd to have you do it, yet I must thank
you both, and own it is now a Genteel pretty
house, and I have no wish but that it was on the
other side Swallow Street, for I would not have
it larger if I could.

Pray take care of Lady Mary . . . and let me
know when you come.

I have nothing to entertain you with here, but
that it is said Lord Euston is to be married
today. It has never come so near the time, but
I have nevertheless heard it doubted, as indeed it
will be till she is seen in her Bridial apparel.
Will you be so good as to tell Mrs. Porter that
the cake and carpet came safe a Wednesday, and
I took the Liberty of taking ye table out of your
Kitchen, there are so many tables at Chicksands you may bring one of those out of the
Gallery. . . . I must beg the favour you will give

the enclosed letter to my Aunt Master yourself, for I would not have my mother see it, therefore pray be carefull, and give it soon, because it wants an answer.

The poor Pilgrims are dismal objects still. Brother Robert Byng (the poor man that is gone) refused £1000 that was offered him for the Living he gave Corbets parson for nothing. Those are offers that are made openly, their being esteemed first fruits. The bond he took was only a form, and which he told Corbets parson he should never take of him, . . . what could be kinder in regard to Corbet, for he knew not the man but by his recomendation . . . but everyone will rail and joyne in beliefe of ill things. Thank God I abominate such easy faith, and never can believe ill of anyone till I am convinced they deserve it! Oh, ungrateful Corbet! for the sake of a dirty parson to spread such faulse reports! . . .

[Before Mrs. Osborn again takes up her pen, her two grandsons, George and John, are born, and the latter event was followed, as related in the Preface, by the death of Lady Mary Osborn in 1743. Lady Ann Jekyll and Lady Betty Archer are her sisters.]

LETTER XXXI.

KENSINGTON, *February* 12, 1744.

Both your boys charming well, George quite in spirits, was to see Lady Ann Jekyll and Lady

Betty Archer yesterday, behaved well at both place.

For Godsake come and see what is doing. The Town is in a turmoil, never was the like, whether truth or not in the reports that are given given about, I know not. The king (George II.) sent a message to the Parliament yesterday that he had undoubted intelligence of the Pretender's son coming to invade these Dominions. You can imagine how this announcement encreases the consternation that is felt,—men, women, not knowing what to believe, such an affright never was before. Upon receiving the king's message, the Duke of Marlborough got up and moved to address the king that they would all stand by him with lives and fortunes. Lord Chesterfield said he was not against that, but desired an Enquiry first from whose ill conduct we were brought to this distress. Lord Lonsdale said "the Enemy was at our Gates. We ought all to be unanimous and not start such things at such a time as this. If a man's house was afire, he must not stay to enquire who did it, but use all means to stop the progress of it," and spoke so strong none pretended to answer him, even made Chesterfield look confounded, and no divisions in that House, but in the Commons was otherways. Pit made the same speach there as Chesterfield did in the other house, but so much more violent, that he was three times caled to order. The Address

was carried 140 majority against 123, but how
Lamentable to think we can have 123 Traytors in
our House.   The Government is rather perplext
with intelligence than satisfyd, for every hour
some or other comes.   Tis certain there are two
ffleets, one at Torbay, the other that was seen
here.   Noris saild a Tuesday to St. Helens, orders
went after him there, and now nobody knows
where he is saild.   Tis said he is gone after
that ffleet off Dunkirk, and that he has been in
sight of ten sail, and fired a gun, but the truth is
not known.   This came from some Pilote.

If Torbay ffleet is the Decoy (for one certainly
is) then they would pour in all men and arms
from Dunkirk, so that our coast would then be
open to them.   Letters have been intercepted
that they are to try to land in Norfolk, Sussex,
Essex or Kent.   The alarm now grows stronger
than it did at first.   There are orders to all officers
to repair to Rendezvous at a moment's warning.   St. James Square, Grosvenor Square, Lin-
colns Inn ffields &c., are appointed.   General
Wentworth went from House of Commons last
night to Harwich to meet the 6000 Dutch troupes
we expect every day.   Tis also said a ship yesterday brought intelligence that several sail of ffrench
passd the Streights of Gibraltar to joyn the
Tholon squadron.   If this is true, they are in
pain, for tis now said there is but a 20 gun frigate
at Dunkirk and some transports.   It is amazing

the different reports that every hour spring up, and tho it appears like men in Buckeram, for here, there and everywhere they see many saile, yet it is quite a serious thing, and every creature in the utmost consternation. I desired brother Robert Osborn to write to you this night if they had any certain intelligence. They live at the office (Admiralty) there are Boards held there sometimes at 4 in the morning. I can tell you no more, but there is a deall to hear.

I am,

your very affec.

S. O.

LETTER XXXII.

[The Mrs. Williamson in this letter was a connection of the Osborns, and her husband was Deputy-Governor of the Tower.]

KENSINGTON, May 29, 1744.

Your boys are both well . . .

Brother Jack insted of being gone again, came to town a Saterday, desires me to make his complyments to you, sorry he just missd of you. Never saw him look better, says the 'Salisbury' has taken good prize, will be two or three thousand pounds, some say five, but it will damp his joy to find Dudley (?) at home. Sure the boy will fly before he comes. I am almost sure I met him on horseback on Kensington Cawsey last Sunday, powdered and spruce. I have seen Mrs.

Williamson, she says every word the Red Ribion
told you is false, and only to shuffle you off from
himself.   Poor Dudley still shews he only went
to a farden school.   For Godsake let all boys
have a propper school till 12 year old at least.
Tis terible to think when they are Captains y‸ it
will be a shame for them to write to the Admiralty.
Poor boys, tis sad when no one belonging to them
think Learning is necessary.   I even am come to
think if they are to be Coblers they should first
go to Westminster.   The officers that last week
went abroad, have had a great escape from being
cut to peices by an Ambuscade of 4000 ffrench,
which was prevented by a Huzar finding it out,
and swam across y‸ river to discover it.   I think
they are all safe arrived at y‸ Army.   Tis sad the
Dutch troops are to return.   Letters yesterday
that Sister George (Byng) mends, tho slow, but
still in a very weak way.

I am,

y‸ truly affect.,

S. O.

LETTER XXXIII.

KENSINGTON, June 20, 1744.

Both boys well, but at present Jack the best,
for tho George is well, yet he has the print of
four fangs in his gums that make him ffretfull
and yallow, and sleep unquiet.   I wish you had
come a week sooner, for he lookd charming.   I

F

cannot say he does so now, tho he was yesterday at Lady Anns (Jekyll). She sent for him. L^y Halifax, Lady Bab and the Burgoynes were there, and they all thought he lookd well, exercisd, and playd with his gun. They were all deverted much, and he behaved very well. The King certainly goes, tho not yet publickly declared, but all things in the family are preparing for it. There is much uneasyness, for we shall be left without King, Army, or ffleet, and the Brest (?) in the Chanel. Ypres is taken, and tis thought Ostend, Nieuport and ffurness will be so by next mail.

You will loose the cream of L^{dl} Anson's History, but if you are happy with y^r haymakers, tis as well. He comes here to-day to kiss hands for his flag. Poor Jack came to town last Tuesday, with his leg on a cushion, and himself bolstered up with pillows in the Coach. I went to him yesterday morning, surprized to see him hopping about ye room. He said he was so at himself, but that the Journey had been of great service, and was so well he would go to Winchester, Anson, &c. I find he was so ill at Portsmouth that no one expected his Life, his going to fetch Anson ashore had like quite to demolish him, oblidged to go to bed that moment, without being able to sup with him, or hear one of his storys. Poor Leg was there, but brim full, for a considerable time held out well, at last the tears ran down. Everyone pittyd him, and did not wonder he should be so moved, for it was impossible to blot out the remembrance of his own fate. Anson looks well, but much thiner, Keppel as brown as a mahogany table.

The ffitzwilliam match is today. Murrays to be at it, therefore Jack's cause cannot be heard which was fixd for to-day. Ffitzwilliam Coach is a curiosity, I think they say it is all Japan.

I dine much at Court, wine in Ice, Creams, &c. Pheasant with Eggs, and Pheasant poults which is shamefull. Dont think but that I can dine on mutton when they are gone. Tomorow I dine with Manchester. Their table is elegant, the ladys I must say is the reverse, tho one may get a dab of Ice there too. Hanover, Montagu, dine with me today. I get a dish or two from the King's kitchen for them.

Now they are come from Court I dont hear a word more to ad, therefore wish you a good Journey, and hope to see you Saterday.

I am,

y^r very affect. mo.

S. O.

LETTER XXXIV.

[The three next letters are full of the panic created by the Young Pretender's Rebellion. Sir Danvers had joined the King's army, under the Duke of Cumberland.]

STRATTON STREET, *Dec.* 9, 1745.

MY DEAR DANVERS,—This will meet you so far south that I find my pen at Liberty to tell you all

I know. First I have the pleasure to tell you both your boys are in perfect health, never had better spirits, . . . tho they have never been out since you went, an odious north-east wind so long that I give them your Apartment below, where they have room for Exercise, and keep quite well.

Your pacquet today in your Bureau I received, and disposd of it as you orderd. I have wrote every post to you, and told you so in one of my letters.

Wednesday last was the most dismal day I ever knew, it being believed here it was the day of Batle, not only myself but every mortal in terror for their ffriends. No one doubted the Rebel Army being beat, but no one knew who would be the perticulers to fall. By ffryday these fears were over, and others succeeded which seizd indeed the whole Town, and was I must say, a most shameful Panick, but the express that came had that effect upon all sorts of people, as it seemd to assure that the Rebels would be at Northampton that night, and in all probability at Barnet a Tuesday. The Councils sat all night, the Army here was forming to march, Lord Stairs was sent to ffinchly to mark out the Camp. The King to head this Army, which people that could keep their senses thought must cut them to peices. One teror added to the rest was a Letter found on Count St Germain, who was taken up, which came from the Rebel Army, and said they hoped they should contrive to slip the Dukes Army, and then make for the Capital. They did not doubt another Army would meet them, but when the King's fforces marched out of London, hoped their friends would have a general mass, and then the four Quarters rise, as he knew all togeather the Consternation of the whole Town is not to be expressd. Thousands of the Pretenders Declarations were threw about the Park and streets, every woman thinking where to run for safty, and every man getting Arms and Horses to go with the King, Brother Torrington among the rest. Lord Shannon was so good to take me and my children to Ashly, thinking cross the water most safe. My Mother to Columbines, Benet to Cooks, Brook Street to Pinkwell. I found a place to hide what was nessessary. Dr Osborn was in town, thought it high time to remove the things from Chicksands. He went down that morning before the consternation was so great and sent Thomas Green with your two Boxes a Sunday, which are now here, and £100 from Denbigh. I beggd the plate to be burried anywhere near him, for imposible to trust that road by the Wagon since we imagind the Highlanders would be at their heals. However Saterday the terors vanishd, and then as sorry to hear the Rebels had gone back. We are all angry with Duke Devonshire, 1000 men that could do nothing, not even take straglers, for we hear they lay down like dogs when they came to Derby, and what up was they to run to Nottingham. In short we now laugh at one another for fearing what was the only thing to destroy them, which was to come on. Lord Sandwich we hear extream ill at Birginham. Lady Sandwich went down in the night a Saterday to him. I pitty you to be a Wagoner at last, however I cant but say I have much better spirits, knowing this will meet you at Woodstock.

No express today of consequence, and yet we flatter ourselves Wade must meet with them in their return, tis shocking to have them go back and reinforce with 3000 ffresh men, which are ready in Scotland.

My Brother Jacks Squadron has taken a ship with 210 men, most of them officers.

The Prisoners came to the Tower a fryday, tis not yet clear if the Pretenders Brother is there. They have strong suspition still, but the Ministry dont choose to talk about it. Mrs Williamson dind with them, and has given me the description. None yet has been sent to see if it is him or not. I fancy it is of no use yet to be sure of it, but we are most dreadfully alarmd at this Embarkation, 14,000 lye at Dunkirk with transports, or rather small ffyshing vessels, and we have a hundred Cutters gone to line all our coasts. 500 seamen came to the Admiralty a Saterday, and they could employ as many more, watermen and all are gone Some think they design to land in Nor-

folk, and that the Rebels intended their march
that way to meet them, but this is all conjecture.
I have only time to give your sons duty to you.
George dreams of you every night, wakes with
telling where you are, and when he heard them
talk of the Pretender coming to St James, he sighd
and said "Where must Aunt Ann go then?"

LETTER XXXV.

LONDON, *December* 10, 1745.

MY DEAR DANVERS,—I wrote you a long scratch
last night at Woodstock which I hope you have
received. I begin this in the morning that I may
have a litle time to tell you of more things than
what concerns rebels. One is that the murrain
amongst the cattel has encreased prodigiously,
that nothing but Mutton can be bought here. I
took the liberty to send for the Hog you had
ffatting at Chicksands, and indeed of most things
we eate from thence, as Butter, bacon, fowls,
greens. Here Rabets are bad and many other
things, so that Mr. Denbigh keeps a seperate
account of all that comes for me, and I have
orderd him to buy more hoggs to ffat, for mutton
soon will be monstrous dear now no one ventures
any other meat in their house. Lambs is fed
with milk. I find it reaches into the Countrys.
Thomas Green says it is among the Cattel at
Baldock from some infected cows that passd there.
It is at Uxbridge and many other places, many of

them that give milk in the morning are dead at
night.   This would be a great Calamity if the
Rebels were not a greater.

Lady Ann has given George a blew and silver
coat, and Jack a pink and silver, much too fine for
them, at least it were now, when there is not a
soul to be seen but in nightgowns and tears.   For
my part I have not stird out of my house since
you went, not even to my mother but of a
Sunday, tho indeed never alone.   If I had any
opposite neighbours, they would think there was
Cabals here, since from eleven in the morning till
12 at night, there is no rest to my doors, some to
tell and some to hear news.   My ffriends I must
say have all been very good to me, tho such a
month as this last have I never passd before.

By your steering to Oxford, I should imagine
you will return to your Bedford station.   I should
realy be glad to know how you and your men do,
for such fatigues I fear, must try your Constitutions.   I pray God Wade may meet with these
Devils that have harazed you all at this rate.

LETTER XXXVI.

STRATTON STREET, *May* 17, 1746.

My boys and I am got here togeather again,
and hope it will not now be long before we see
you.   Lady Anne told me yesterday she heard
the new Regiments would be broke next week,

tho her news is not always certain.   The Dukes [1]
Answers to both Lords and Commons are much
spoke off as being extremely well, with a very
modest and pretty turn in them.   If they are
printed, you shall have them.   I received your
Letter yesterday with that Perticuler enclosed
which you desire to be put in your Scrutore
(Escritoire ?).   I have the key, and shall do it
tomorrow.   I shall send down the writings to
Doctor Osborn next Wednesday.   John being still
lame makes me behindhand in some of your
orders. . . . The musick shall go too if posible.

I have not missd one post writeing, therefore
tho you had none the day you wrote, yet I hope
it came to you by the next.   Tho George is well
to me, yet if you see him soon you will be
frighted, for he is not the same Child, and most
monstrously disguised by a Wig he has got on
to-day.   His hair is cut quite close, and as soon
as his head can be shaved, it must be so, and his
eyebrows too.   He walks like a rickety child, in
short I dont wish you to see him this two months,
even his voice is quite alterd, and does not speak
so plain as when you left him, but all these things
are common from the weakness his Ilness reduced
him too.   He has as good if not better spirits
than ever, but is very pevish.   Jack looks like a
ghost, but yet he is bright and in good spirits,
and they say time will bring it all right again. . . .

[1] Duke of Cumberland.

The Burgoynes look as bad, and so indeed do the ffieldings, they lodge next door to us here. They lay great fault upon Sir Roger—they are all gone down to Sutton.

I am, y^r very affec.,

S. O.

LETTER XXXVII.

KENSINGTON, *June* 14, 1746.

The wind is still in the Duke of Bedfords teeth, and he no farther than Yarmouth. It also keeps the Prince of Hesse here, he does not go till he hears his Troupes are Landed. He is called the drop to Lady Rochfords earring.

Thursday last was expected to be a day of Batle in the House of Lords on sending our Troupes abroad, but there proved to be only two speakers. Lord Lonsdale, who spoke an hour against it, and was so well answered by the Duke of Newcastle, that no one else attempted to say more, and the expected long day proved to be a very short one.

Tis thought twill be August before the Lords can be tryd. After some forms are past, the Peers must have 20 days notice. Lady Cromarty is in town, has been at the Tower to enquire after her Lord. She was at Williamsons, and cryd most bitterly, but no one is sufferd so much as to look up at the windows. They were all

brought into Williamsons, and from thence one
by one conducted to their appartment. No one
knows where the other is, and they are kept
prodigious strict. Sure the King of ffrance has
orderd a most insolent Letter, and takes himself
to be King of England, to forbid our punishing
the Rebels.

Is the Pretender got off or not? I wish they
could have been beheaded at Edinburgh, and not
make such a long peice of work as the forms will
do here, tis thought the Parliament will set till
August. I was not used to a Lodging, and
therfore not aware how sharp they are, but
found my bills most immoderate, which my people
told me they could not turn their backs but meat,
bread, butter, &c., was stole away. I really
believe they have keys themselves to take what
is lockd when they have oppertunity. There
was only ye woman and girl in the house, but her
husband and family live vere near, and I daresay
was all kept, but when mother was to come, I
askd if she would leave the house to us, which
she did, and now she is out, I shall keep her so
after mother goes, for it was intollerable. Indeed
I believe it would have been much cheaper to have
gone to Chicksands, eight guineas for lodging, and
living has been very dear ever since we came.

Your son George lost his heart yesterday. A
miss who came to visit next door, came in the
Garden to him. He lookd at her first with sur-

prise, then slyly lead her to the Arbor where I
was setting, and desired me to set her up by him,
which I did.   After he had looked at her some
time, he strokd her face, and kissd her, he then
shewd her his watch, gatherd a rose, and brought
it to her.   You would have dyed with laughing
to see the courtship.   There was another girl not
half so handsome, he never took the least notice
of her, but Jack kissd them both, and was happy
with either.   As soon as George was up this
morning, he desired to go into the garden to see
if miss was there, a good fine girl indeed she is.

By a letter from Bath, Aunt Ann Master is
better already, all the yellow gone from her eyes
and skin. . . . I hope she will do well, her Loss
would be irreparable to my mother, who is chearfull and easy here, tho a sad place for her to be in.
There was a farmhouse that with a coach would
have been very agreeable, but without one very
inconvenient.   I now wish to have it, but it is let.
We go out airing every day, and your boys
with us. . . .

LETTER XXXVIII.

[This letter is written immediately after the death of
Sarah's brother George, third Viscount Torrington.   The
"Brother Byng" referred to is her youngest brother
Edward.   "Daniel" is probably a brother of George's
widow, whose family name it was.   It appears that
Lord Torrington in his will has bequeathed the London

house to her, and Sarah is indignant that her mother should, at her age, be forced to give it up. She writes to Sir Danvers to beg him to use his influence on her behalf.]

STRATTON STREET, *April* 8, 1750.

I cannot help sending to you. My Brother Byng came to town this morning, seems much out of sorts that he is not namd, is glad you are, that some one who has regard for the family is, outragious that the house is given to sister to have it took from Mother for that purpose. Daniel I fear has been too stiff with him. He askd Daniel what was Mother to do. He said he did not know. " Sure she is not to be turnd out when she can live so short a time." He said house was to be let.

For God sake make my sister and Daniel sensible they should not disoblidge him. He seems varstly netled with Daniel. I think he will act the lawyer and not the gentleman. Sure they must live as they do for at least one twelve-month, some credit to be thought off, some decency in regard to my mother. She should not be tossd about, cannot live long. Brother Byng talks of going down soon again, and therefore I do this that you may prepare Daniel, for if he and sister do not think it worth while to oblidge and give way in some measure, Bro. Byng will forget he has that nephew. As he says, his Brother forgot there was such an individual as himself.   They may endeavour, but it will not be posible to let the house, they should at least offer him to be the person.   He would like it I dare-say, on his own terms, which would be perhaps, to keep it up, and he would keep Mother in it, at least till farther consideration.   Let sister go to Yotes if she likes it, but Mother must not be disgracefully hurried about.   Daniels surly temper will ruin his nephew, if he dont take care.   You must soften it.

Are your boys to have grey, and who must make it for them?   George puts on the man I assure you, looks and is very well.   He set down imediatly to write this as soon as he came home.   He got a gramar in your room, and all done before I saw it, ruled it himself as you see, and being so awry, I ruled a paper for him, and he wrote it again this morning.   He will go to Mrs. Hawkins tonight—says he got a place by telling a boy a word he did not know.

For God sake take care Mother.   Consider she is 80.   Aunt Martha very ill, St. Anthonys fire.

I am, yʳ very affect.,

S. O.

LETTER XXXIX.

LONDON, *October* 14, 1750.

Chicksands Affaires.

Halkins and Pears have finishd all you orderd. The roof could not be done before Harvest, the fear of weather spoiling the ceilings oblidged me to let them be ten days in the Harvest to finish it.

The Bedchamber, drawingroom, and antyroom floors are laid, but not planed, as there will be whitewashing and painting, &c., next year. Everyone and even Pears himself said it was better it should be the last thing done. The staires are done, and Brome Closet put up on them, also the Corner Dressingroom, and bords put to the windows there. The antiroom and drawingroom chimneys are finished, and all the windows as you orderd. The antiroom chimney does not smoke, the other I did not try.

The chimney wall in the little green room was not dry enough to put up the green paper.

The Tapistry is packd up in the Gallery for you to approve. I could not undertake to finish it without your oppinion. There is enough for one side and both ends, and if you would give up any carpets, near half enough for the other side. Bradshaw says he has some will match y^t will come as cheap as paper. The pictures are all collected together and packd up in the antiroom, except the one over your Harpsichord, which I did not care to remove. Lady Temple is there, also the Scripture piece removed from this parlour, and from being a cut-throat room, will I daresay when finished, be the most agreeable one in the house. Many that were at Chicksands this summer said that $\frac{1}{2}$ length philosopher, as we calld it, was a very good one. A person who knew it said it was Dun Scotus, a very learned man, who livd in the 14 Century, as is known by manuscript of his own at Oxford.

There is no tapistry behind the Reformers in the Bedchamber, therefore they remain as they were.

The Library is very well cleand, some books there was spoilt with mould.

Murthers od Jobs were double what you expected, and the Carpender did not end till Michaelmas day, and came to more also, the one 3 shillings and the other 4 shillings. Extraordinary. No fresh order to either, only finishd what you orderd. All is paid to the day I came away, and no Workman left there.

I sent George up with George Byng, who came down with him, and spent the Holydays at Chicksands. Lord Torrington, Robert Byng and Bullock, and K. Scott were at Southill, so they all came and went together, and was exact to the school time. I stayd a fortnight after to see all clean. Everything left perpectly so when I came away, but you must not expect it will keep from vermin without a maid in it. Mary Meagar who married from me last year has offerd her services, and was when with me a very good servant, but I could say to her no more than that . . . I would recommend her if you took any one. Indeed your house will suffer more than six times her wages, and even now that only four men are left, they must hire to wash, etc.

19 *July*. Nat went to Southill at six in the morning to have Toby shod. A shepherd and dog came short from a hedg upon him, he started and threw the boy, who lay some time not able to stir. The horse ran away, got his foot in the bridle which throwd him down just at Southill gate. Cut his knees terribly, not able for Mr. Denbigh to ride till the week I came away.

The same evening Thom Green rode Magot to water, and led the blind one, who soon began to plunge and turn round several times (has done so before in the stable, and had been blooded). Green at last oblidged to quit the halter. The workmen and all ran to help, but could not save him or get him out till he was dead. The same day the grey horse was taken with a fever. Ben Squire attended him 3 weeks and then he dyed. Many people lost horses, such heat was hardly ever rememberd, and they would work them in the midle of the day as usal. I then said we should kill all the horses if they would do so, but women are fools. I am unlucky in foreseeing events I cannot prevent. The workmen tyling, were like poor Creatures on a Gridyron, so spent, oblidged to change the hours, and work early and late, Nutkins himself at 2 in the morning. But the poor horses could not groan out their suffering. Such extreme heat for so long were very unusal.

LETTER XL.

[This letter is in the form of a Journal, and relates all events between May and October 1750.]

June 23.—Captain Sheldon took a house ready furnished at Ampthill for six guineas a year.

July 6.—Mr. Pecks dyed of a mortification, lifting a person over a gate. Her pocket hitched upon it, which he prest upon to prevent her falling, and a small key burst through his body.

July 10, 11, 13.—The most extream heat ever known in England, and indeed for ten days continued to a high degree.

July 16.—The most terible thunder and lightening I ever heard. Hailstones as large as pigeons eggs, some at Shefford three inches round.

Aug. 1.—Lady Torrington a month at Yotes, her mother ill, but old women dont dye.

Aug. 8.—Duke of Richmond dyed of violent fever, twas said from the excessive heat at Installation. He has left all his houses and everything to the Dutches. Mr. ffox has behaved like an angel to her, shared all her afflictions and troubles. [Mr. Fox, afterwards Lord Holland, had married the Duke's second daughter.] Such maloncholy scenes

have been there, is not to be repeated.
How short is our Light! The daughter
[Duchess of Leinster] married to ambitious
views is a thorn in her side, while that which
disoblidged her, and was never to expect
forgiveness, turns out her great and only
comfort, both her and him showing the
greatest tenderness.

Aug. 14.—Admiral Byng thrown down in
his park by a buck . . . now gone to Bath,
and surprizingly recovered.

Brother Peter Osborn is 2nd Captain of
Greenwich Hospital, £200 a year, an apartment there, coals, candle, brooms, etc. Prince
and Princess of Wales three days at Portsmouth Dock. They were highly honourd
by their civilitys, left 30 gineas to the servants.

Sep.—Mr. Alston to marry Miss Bovey.
She is 19, has £1500 a year, and £10,000
in money, which Sir Rowland takes and
setles Odell and £1700 a year in present.
Land wont pay batchelor Debts, and od Jobs,
weding expenses, and fit up Odel, and then
must be crampt for life. An Upholster was
sent down to ffurnish her house at Slow,
where they are at present.

Harry Legg married to Lord Stowels
daughter, at present Heiress Aparent to
£6000 a year.

Burgoyn has the Measels at Eton, is now

brought down to Sutton, very far from well.

Earthquakes in Northamptonshire, Leicestershire, and the adjacent Counties. Lord Halifax felt it at Horton, Lord Northampton at his house, Mr. Wright at his. No damage done, but it is very unpleasent to find the earth as unquiet as ourselves. I am very sure it was about the same time at Chicksands, none but my self awake in the house, and therefore none sensible of it, the Jog and Ratle of the Windows the same of that in London. I own I was alarmd, got up and found it 2 o'clock, but none else has yet said it was felt in Bedfordshire.

Oct^r.—Lady Caroline Collier to have Sir Nathanael Carsons son. Lathams mother dead and Medcalf aunt. Eldest Miss Hotham dead.

Lady Hervey and her son, the Captain, gone to live at Paris, taken a house for 2 year. I wish I could buy her house in the Park, they say it is to be sold. You will think it a mad wish.

Lord and Lady Halifax in town, neither of them well.

Lady Ann and her dear gone a progress into the North. Lumley Castle designd for Scotland, but I hear are returning.

Lady Betty in Warwickshire very far from well.

Lady Bab at Bath, her Miss Robinsons Mr. Scot is made Preceptor to Prince George, and tis said Lord North his Governor, but I am told he is not to be calld so, and sure upon no other foot he can serve him.

The Doctor (Osborn) is going the high road after his sister Betty if some care is not taken, he ownd to me his Life was a burden he was not able to bear, and many things when we meet will confirm my fears. Love and preferment on the foundations. God knows how it will end. Something should be done to take him from the present scene.

One of the Wandesford's married, the other going to live with Sister Margaret. Southill, Bennet Street, and all else I think as you left them, as is

yr. affect.

Tis thought the King will be here next month, and no Parliament till after Xmas. The town is a desart, therefore see no Creature that knows truth.

Lord Plymouth married, poor girl, is it posible she can be happy? Your boys both very well, long for your return, send Duty.

Mr. Beacher struck with dead palsie the day before I left Bedfordshire, but dont hear yet he is dead.

I forget if Brownsel dyed before you went, and left all to Orlebar.

You dont like letters, therefore only send you a sort of Journal.

LETTER XLI.

STRATTON STREET, *April* 9, 1751.

George has been extremely ill since Sunday. I could no longer than that day defer sending for Cox.   Both he and I, who indeed have no judgment, thought him very bad . . . he greatly relievd him, . . . at night he was blisterd and is better today, and at present in no danger, tho not yet able to Lift his head from the pillow.

This has been repeated neglected colds.   Two guineas a month ago had saved many now, for this is attended with much expence.   Cox has had 3 guineas already, and been here twice a day for it.   Guy and Hicks with blisters, Bleeding, etc.   Latham's illness has been terrible too, and most unlucky at this time, not yet out of her bed, except an hour or two in the day.   Master John has a dreadfull hourse Cough, but hope to prevent his being ill.   Asses milk has already made him better, and no one able to be about them but my self, who should be in bed too, if old fashion affection did not keep me in their service, for there is much more to do than you imagine. George is in your bed, Jack in mine.   Sister

Margaret Osborn set up last night, and today I
have got Sympson, for I have not been in bed
two hours at a time these 5 nights. Tis unlucky to employ so many people, but no remedy
now. All this will incur your farther displeasure,
but I am unable to help it. When they are in
other hands, I hope many expenses will be saved,
tho I wish you may not find experiments of their
Constitutions fatal.

I am, y^r affect.

S. O.

LETTER XLII.

STRATTON STREET, *May* 28, 1751.

The duel which was in the papers last Saturday is a most malancholy affaire. Mr. Dalton
was very soon to marry one of the Miss Greens,
and a snuff box which he had given her was
taken from her by Mr. Paul, who told her she
took so much snuff that he would keep it.
Dalton said he insisted he should not, but give
it to him, so from Jest to Earnest wrested it out
of his hand, and Miss Green had her box returnd. At night Paul went to Dalton's house in
Hill Street, not finding him at home, he sat down
in his Parlour, wrote a letter in which he said he
had used him ruffley, and that he expected he
should ask his pardon, or give him satisfaction
like a gentleman, and sent his Servant with it
where he suppd, and to say that he should wait

there till he came home, which he immediately did. Both their chairs waited at the door, and they sent the Servant to stay in the Kitchen till they calld, and not to let anyone in that knockd. Dalton said, if they must fight, the present time was best, so drawd their swords. In the scufle the Candles and Tables were thrown down, and one of them said, "Don't let us fight in the dark, peace till we fetch the Candle out of the Hall," but it was soon over, and Paul went out of the door, gave his chairmen 2 shillings to discharge them, and went for Hawkins the surgeon (the only circumstance in his favour) to go for Dalton, for he believd he had killd him, then run to Lord Ravensworth to tell him his misfortune, who advised him to get off directly. Tis only from what he told Lord Ravensworth that the above perticulers are known, for the poor man never spoke. Upon the street door shutting, the Servant ran up, found his master stone dead upon the flour. He ran to Mr. Wright in Groves Street, who was Daltons uncle, they sent for Midleton, who came ten minits before Hawkins, therefore suspected Paul did not go to Hawkins till he was advised to do so. They found the Challenge in Dalton's pocket, and the appearance of a very unfair Wound, it being on the contrary side of his heart and lungs. The swords both lay by him. Dalton's was much hackd, and all Tallow. He knew nothing of a sword, and the other fenced well, nevertheless most people think he had the mortal wound after he was down, tho the Surgeons endeavour to make it posible to be otherways.   The Coroners Inquest was not finished till last night, and brought it in Wilfull Murder.

Daltons father lost another son this week of the small pox, and Miss Green has neither shut her eyes, or spoke since. I pitty Paul's parents, but he did this too premeditated to escape hanging.

Miss Bishopp is to have Sir William Maynhard. He setles very handsom, desires no present fortune, but to have her share with the others when Sir Cecil dyes. I daresay she will make him a good wife.   Gratitude ought to make her do it.

This is Sir Cecils lucky year.   His mother has dyed, by whom he has got £2000 a year, he has also a place of £500 a year in ye Ordanance, his son Page to the Prince of Wales, and his daughter to be soon so well married.

Large familys in general are more lucky than small ones.   Too much anxiety is not pleasing to Heaven, I hardly ever knew it succeed.   Self, self, self can never prosper, for Happyness or Content is not to be purchased by Money.

LETTER XLIII.

LONDON, *June* 19, 1751.

George is as much better as posible.   He set in my Dressingroom yesterday, and today has

been in the Park, is weak but well, eates and
sleeps, and therefore I hope will be fit for school
Sunday evening.   I went to Westminster last
night, found poor Jack in tears, had been taken
ill about half an hour. . . . I am an unfortunate mortal, always run into the mouth of some
ill luck or other, and therefore instink carryd me
down to see him—you three divide my heart,
therefore if you think I shall be too far from them,
I will not go to Brother Byng this summer.

I conclude I may send for Master John to
dinner on Sunday.   I shall send again to know
how he is.

I am y^r affect.

S. O.

I have seen the plan of Lord Berkeleys
Ground.   It is 120 feet deep, and Stables is
to be where Philips says, but you see I pay the
ground rent of those stables. . . .

George is gone, sends his Duty, but says he
must not write to you till Saterday.

LETTER XLIV.

STRATTON STREET, June 29, 1751.

Both your sons are very well, I sent John this
evening.   They dine at Sister Byngs tomorrow.
I conclude you gave them order if you would have
them write to you.

Mr. King, my landlord, has his new house just

finished, entirely burnt down, tis thought to be maliciously done. I suppose the workmen were disoblidged that he had not been generous to them. Tis terible we are brought to be subject to the mob.

Lord Tilney went from Wansted, as his family thought to London for a few days, but he wrote to his sister from thence that he was going to Paris and perhaps to Italy for three years. The town says he is gone with Lord Southwell and Strickland to Spaa, and that they will fill their pockets before they part with him.

The Princess of Wales returns to Leicester House tomorrow.

I am, y^r affect.

S. O.

LETTER XLV.

STRATTON STREET, July 30, 1751.

MY DEAR DANVERS,—I have a persentiment of coming evil . . . to our family, why I know not, but tis to be hoped I am mistaken. We have had enough, God knows, but if it comes, we must meet it with fortitude and resignation. At present we are all well here.

Lord and Lady Torrington and Daniel came to Kit's End by ten a Sunday, and he stayd there last night, and dind with Sister Torrington at Hendon. Tis to be much hoped that they went on well together, and that she held her tongue in check. Women somtimes find it hard to do so, they say, tho I dont find it so.

Sister Torrington is again ill with some distressing indisposition, kept her bed Saterday and Sunday, but is better. Sister Torrington returnd to Southill today in Brothers Chariot to Stevenage, but they would not let her go alone, so Ned, tho very bad, was goodnatured and went with her. They were to take postchaise from Stevenage, and after he had baited himself and horses, he returns the same way to Stevenage, and then in Brothers Chariot home.

I cannot say Sister Margaret Osborn met with so much complaisance, for the Doctor forgot to send his Chariot, that when she came to Wellwyn she was distressd, and oblidged to take a postchaise to Stevenage, and there was none to come farther, but one that the poor horses were just come in and tyerd. However she and the postillions came along, and I suppose she had not a joyful meeting with the Doctor, for both would be out of humour. I must say it was a very disagreeable thing to go alone in that manner, but there is a ruffness in the blood of the Osborns that one does not generally meet with. Duke of St. Albans dyed a Saterday. Some give the Constable of Windsor to the Duke, as it greatly interferes with the fforest, and all his Teritorys there about.

There is not a silable of news, at least that I hear. The Town is now empty, and I have not

seen a soul except Brother Byng.   This morning
he brought nephew Torrington as he was carrying him to school.   He desired me to say that he
fears Joynes has forgot the model of your large
roler, he beggs you will refresh his memory.

He believes he shall go to Southill for few days
at Bartholomews, to carry the boy, and then he will
give him somthing, but he did not bid me say so.

You will be tyerd reading nonsense from
> your very affec. Mother,
> > S. O.

LETTER XLVI.

CHICKSANDS, *September* 3, 1751.

The reason I trouble you with this is only being
Brother Byngs secretary.   He intends spending
a week at Southill, and my sister Byng is to go
with him there.   If it suit your schemes to have all
the boys come up as they went down, he will pay
half the Coach, and sister and he go down in it to
Southill.   This is no proposition of mine, and I
wish they would write their own letters, and not
trouble me with what I have nothing to do.

He also desires to know what day you fix for
the boys to come, that they may be ready to
your time.   They propose a postchaise back to
Stevenage, but that I have no commission to say,
and indeed needless to ad that a large coach and
cold weather Latham might squeeze in.   To
oblidge you I shall not be of their partie.   I

wish you would let George ad in his letter to me that you had received Hardings note from me. . . .

Sunday Brother Edward went to Kits End for some time, and I with him for a few hours visite. I never see the owner better, quite happy there, talks of keeping it warm the whole winter, spends his time chearfull, and comfortable with his Old Dame as he calls her. Whats matter what it is? If people can be happy at pushpin, tis as entertaining to them as the most refind satisfaction to those of a more exalted genius. Since happyness is not confind to any situation, and it is a very vain pursuit, I conclude it praiseworthy to let the mind fall till it sinks into nothing, and forget what God created us for.

Poor Edward I left there, I think worse than ever I saw him. He says he went ill to Danbury, and was so all the time he was there. I am sure was very bad all the week he was in town, . . . cannot eate, or has strength or spirit left. Wether the Old Dame can nurse him up or not I cannot say, but tis maloncholy to see him so. Insted of growing hardend as I grow older, I every day find myself less fit for this world. Such a crowd of disagreeable reflections pressd upon me as I returnd from my visite, that I cannot even yet shake off the effect of it from my mind.

I am and must ever be,

your very affectionate Mother,

S. Osborn.

Lady Pembroke to marry Captain Barnet of the Gards, a very agreeable man, some thousands less than nothing, but her lord left her £1200 to assist him.   Thanks for the cowcumbers.

LETTER XLVII.

STRATTON STREET, *Oct.* 3, 1751.

I believe I shall not set out for Southill till near Wednesday, unless worse letters should come from there, so that if it is convenient to you to send a horse for John to Hatfield on Tuesday, I should be oblidged to you, but don't do it without it is so. If we find one there, it is well ; if not, that will be well too.   What slow journeys we make in these days !   It takes days to get to where our wishes are to be.   Will it always be so ?

Poor Edward still ill . . . tis shocking to see all our family going before one.   How few left !

The Admiral here, and pretty well, desires me to ad his respects, with the affection of

yours,

S. O.

I am now 58 yeares old, wishing time to be no more, but that must be as Heaven decrees.

[This is the last letter of Mrs. Osborn to her son. Indeed, it is the last letter of hers for nearly fifteen years. Sir Danvers died in 1753, and the next time Sarah resumes her pen, it is to address her grandson. But before passing on to this period, it becomes necessary to introduce the sad story of her unfortunate brother, Admiral Byng.]

Although the trial and execution of Admiral Byng are matters of history, and as such are familiar to most of us, it will not be thought out of place to give here a brief account of the circumstances connected with them.   In the year 1756, when repeated advice had been received at London that the French meditated a descent upon the island of Minorca, Admiral Byng was selected to command a fleet for the defence of that place. I quote the rest from Macaulay, who was a warm partisan of the Admiral's, and defended his conduct throughout.   " The Admiral . . . did not think fit to engage the French squadron, and sailed back without having effected his purpose. The people were inflamed to madness . . . the city of London called for vengeance . . . the people were not in a mood to be trifled with . . . their cry was for blood."

Minorca fell into the hands of the French, and Admiral Byng was brought back to England, tried by court martial, acquitted of the charges of cowardice and disaffection, but convicted of an error in judgment.   He was sentenced to be shot, but with a strong recommendation to mercy.   In spite of the popular clamour against him, a large number of people espoused his cause, and threw the blame of the disaster on the Ministry, for

The Hon. John Byng Esq. — Admiral of the Blue.
fourth Son of the Right Honourable — LORD VISCOUNT TORINGTON.
Who Unfortunately suffer'd on Board the — Monarque y 14 Day of March in ye Year 1757.
... From an Original in ye Possession — of the Hon. Mr. Osborn ...

Vain in the Portrait, Friendship seeks Relief. — The pencild Phantom yet thy Foes shall Awe
Where Semblance serves but to perpetuate Grief. — Whose Blood proclaims their Martyrdom of Law.

having provided him with a fleet quite inadequate
to the task imposed on him. Pitt pleaded his
cause in person with the King, and reported that
the House of Commons seemed inclined to mercy.
Macaulay gives the King's answer. "Sir," he
said, "you have taught me to look for the sense
of my people in other places than the House of
Commons." It was evident that there was to be
no reprieve for Byng, and his sentence was carried
out on March 14, 1757, on board the *Monarque*,
where he met his fate with great courage. The
accompanying testimonial to his reputation, written
to M. Voltaire by the Duke of Richlieu, who
commanded the French forces on that occasion,
in which he asserts that the English fleet would
have certainly been destroyed had it persisted in
an attack, is of great weight as coming from so
competent a judge.

M. Voltaire himself enclosed it to Admiral
Byng, and the letter is dated January 2nd, 1757,
written from his retreat at Les Delices, near
Geneva. The original is at Chicksands Priory.

SIR,—Tho' I am almost unknown to you, I
think tis my duty to send you the copy of the
letter which I have just received from the
Marshall Duke of Richlieu. Honour, humanity,
and equity order me to convey it into your hands.
This noble and unexpected testimony from one of
the most candid, as well as the most generous of

my countrymen, makes me presume your Judges will do you the same justice.

I am, with respect,

your most humble obedient Servant,

VOLTAIRE.

Copy of the Duc de Richlieu's letter, written at Paris, December 26, 1756.

"Le sort de l'Amiral Byng me fait grand pitié. Je vous assure que tout ce que j'a vû et scû de lui ne devoit tourner qu' à sa gloire : elle ne doit point être attaquée quand on a été battû, après avoir fait tout ce qu'on pouvoit attendre. Il faut bien que quand deux honnêtes gens se battent, il y en ait un qui oie du Desavantage, sans que cela lui faire tort. Toutes les manœuvres de l'Amiral Byng ont été admirables, au dire naturel de tous nos marines, les Forces étoient au moins égalles, puis que les Anglois avoient treize Vaisseaux, et que nous en avions douze avec des Equipages plus nombreux et plus fraix. Le Hazard qui préside à tous les combats, et surtout à ceux de mer, nous fut plus favorable en envoyant plus de nos Boulets dans les Manœuvres des Anglois, et il me semble qu'il est generallement reconnû qui si les Anglois s'étoient obstinés, leur Flotte auroit été perdue, de sorte qu'il n'y a jamais en d'Injustice plus criante que celle qu'on voudroit faire à l'Amiral Byng, et tout nomme d'honneur et tout militaire surtout doit s'y interresser."

Marshal Richlieu and Monsieur Voltaire both received an acknowledgment of their kindness from Admiral Byng before his death. It was in reference to Admiral Byng that Voltaire made his well-known remark, that he was condemned to be shot "pour encourager les autres." Another tribute to his memory was that of the sailor, who, on seeing his dead body, exclaimed, " There lies the best and bravest officer of the navy."

The three following documents, consisting of two letters written by Mrs. Osborn to the Duke of Bedford, and also her appeal to the Lords of the Admiralty, I have the permission of the present Duke of Bedford to include in this volume, as well as the Duke's reply to her first petition, which was very guarded in his promise of assistance.

[Copy.]

CHARLES STREET, BERKELEY SQUARE,
Feb. 5, 1757.

My LORD,—The present distress of our family must plead with your Grace for my attempting to intrude on your quiet hours at Wooburn, to represent our own melancholy situation, tho my unhappy Brother's fate will, I hope, sufficiently justify an application to one of the Duke of Bedford's character, even yet I should not have dared to have troubled your Grace, were not

my Brother's sufferings already such, as scarce
any crime could have imposed. Ignominiously
suspended, most ignominiously aspersed, and in-
humanely traduced, throughout the World, on
suppositions which his family must have shared
the disgrace of, and from which not even his
father's services to this nation could have afforded
a shadow of refuge, had they not been as amply
disproved, and he as justly acquitted of.

Under these Circumstances, may I implore
your Grace to consider the Sentence he lyes
under, which is generally thought as Illegal as
Severe — my nephew Torrington has therefore
venturd to Petition the King in his favour, and
as we are informed this extraordinary case may
be referd to the Cabinet Council, we hope it will
be at a time when your Grace is present, if we
are so fortunate as to have that so, we entreat
your compassion, and known disposition to Justice
may Unite in Leaning towards that Mercy which
has been so earnestly recommended by the Court
Martial. Your Grace's family lost one of the
noblest blossoms from unjust Oppression, to whom
then can I better address myself than to one, who
in every Action of Life has show'd a detestation
of it in what-soever shape it has appeared.

Pitty, my Lord, a distressed Sister, surrounded
only by weeping females, and helpless Boys, who
will all owe gratefull acknowledgements of their
future happyness to the influence the Duke of

Bedford must always have, when Justice and Mercy are the objects of his care.

I am, my Lord Duke,

Your Grace's most obedient Servant,

(Signed)   S. OSBORN.

The above is extracted from Bedford Papers, vol. xxxiii. fol. 67. To which the answer was as follows :—

MADAM, — I am but just able, thro' extreme weakness of my right Hand occasioned by the Gout, to acknowledge the receipt of your letter. All I can at present say in answer to it, is, that in case His Majesty shall be pleased to refer the sentence of the Court Martial to His Cabinet Council, nothing but absolute incapacity on account of health shall prevent my attending it, and I shall be very happy if upon a strict exa-mination into the proceedings of the Court Martial, I shall find myself at liberty to adopt those sentiments of mercy which that Court has so strongly recommended to His Majesty, as no one has a more real regard for yourself and Lord Torrington and his family than myself.

I am, your sincere and humble Servant,

BEDFORD.

[Copy.]

Extracted from the Bedford Papers, vol. xxxiii. fol. 86.

MY LORD,—Your Grace's friendly reception of me the other day, and the concern you was pleased to express for my unfortunate Brother, encourages me to enclose to your Grace the Letter I sent yesterday to the Lords of the Admiralty as the last efforts with their Lordships that an unhappy sister can make.   The reasons I have troubled them with in my Brother's behalf are briefly stated, but I hope your Grace will think they have their weight ; indeed, my Lord, it is terrible to think of my poor Brother's execution being orderd in consequence of a sentence in a great degree appeald from by those who passd it, not understood by the world, and passd under a Law doubtfull and unexplained.   The hardship of my Brother's approaching fate is every hour more and more felt, tho' I have never yet heard of the Case having been laid before his Majesty with the alleviating circumstances that attend it.   A cruel and false notion that his Majesty is disinclyned to mercy on this occasion has probably prevented it.

I have no right, God knows, my Lord, to ask any such favour of your Grace, but as you are a Friend to Justice, to truth and to mercy, and if I may venture to add, a friend to our afflicted family, I flatter my self that any steps your Grace shall think propper to take in the obtaining his Majesty's mercy, or at least, clearing up this dark affair, may at the same time, as it saves my innocent Brother's Life, to which tho' he himself may be indifferent, his unfortunate sister wishes to preserve, may do eternal honour to your Grace's Name.

It may be propper to inform your Grace that Admiral fforbes refused signing the order for execution, and has given given Lord Temple his reasons in writing for such refusal which he has desired him to lay before the King.

I am,

my Lord Duke,

your Grace's most Oblidged and obedient

Humble Servant,

(Signed)   S. Osborn.

Charles Street, Berkeley Square,
    ffryday morning, *Feb.* 18.

Copy of a Letter inclosed in that of the Honble Mrs. Osborn (dated Feb. 18, 1757), relating to Admiral Byng's sentence :—

My Lords,—The Judges having reported to his Majesty in Council, that the sentence passed on my unfortunate Brother is a legal one, permit me to implore your Lordships' Intercession with his Majesty for his most gracious mercy, and to hope your Lordships will not think an afflicted sister's application ill founded in a case so hardly circumstanced, and which the Judges (tho' by the Severity of the Law they have thought themselves obliged to pronounce the fatal Sentence) have recommended to your Lordships' Humanity, to the Justice I will not presume to add ; tho' in their Letter to your Lordships they say that in

Justice to the Prisoner as well as for their own conscience's sake they recommend him to his Majesty's mercy.

The Court Martial, my Lords, seem to have acquitted my unhappy Brother of Cowardice and disaffection, and therefore it is presumed he stands sentenced under the Head of Negligence. It is not fitting perhaps that a wretched woman as I am should offer any Arguments in my Brother's Behalf to yr Lordships, who are Masters of the whole, but what Criminal Negligence, my Lords, can there have been in which neither Cowardice nor Disaffection have had a part? What Criminal Negligence can there have been since the Judges have thought it incumbent on them for their own Conscience's sake and in Justice to the prisoner to recommend him to his Majesty's Mercy? I must submit to your Lordships whether it be the meaning of the Law that every kind of Negligence wilfull, or not, should be punished with death, if so, it is not for me to make an Observation on the Laws, if not, and Negligence arising neither from Cowardice, Disaffection, or Wilfulness, ought not according to the Spirit and Intention of the Law to be deem'd Capital, why, my Lords, should my poor Brother suffer, when both the Sentence by which he is condemned and the Letter to yr Lordships by which he is so strongly recommended to his Majesty's Mercy fully prove that his Judges do not deem him deserving of the punishment they thought themselves obliged to sentence him to.

I hope your Lordships will not think he ought to suffer either under a Law unexplain'd or doubtful, or under a Sentence erroneously passed, if the Law has been misunderstood, and my unfortunate Brother hath been condemned under the 12th Article according to the Spirit and meaning of which he should not have been condemned, I submit to your Lordships whether his Life should be the Forfeit.

If there is a Doubt on the principles and motives that induced the Court Martial to intreat the Intercession of yr Lordships with his Majesty for Mercy, I submit to your Lordships, whether those motives should not be more fully explain'd before it be too late. It would be needless to mention the usual course of his Majesty's mercy to the condemned upon the application of his Judges; if my unhappy Brother's case had circumstances particularly unfavourable in it, but as on the contrary for the Reasons I have ventur'd briefly to offer, and the many others that must occur to your Lordships, his case appears to be uncommonly hard and well deserving of that mercy to which his Judges have so earnestly recommended Him, I hope I shall stand excused if I beseech your Lordships' immediate Intercession with his Majesty in his behalf.—I am, &c.

Extracted from the Bedford Papers, vol. xxxiii. p. 88.

Admiral Byng's last letter to his sister, dated March 12, 1757, is endorsed in her handwriting, thus :—

My brother from on board the Monarque, the last letter from him, the 14th being the fatal day appointed for him to dye, to the Perpetual disgrace of Publick Justice.

MY DEAR, DEAR SISTER,—I can only with my last breath thank you over and over again for all your endeavours to serve me in my present Situation.   All has proved fruitless, but nothing wanting in you that could be done.   God for ever bless you is the sincere prayers of your most affec^t Bro.

J. BYNG.

Inclosed I send you a receipt for Bro. Edward's legacy, which you will do me the favor to accept of as a small Token of my affection to you.

The succeeding document is also endorsed by Mrs Osborn with these words : "The original paper wrote by my unfortunate and injur'd Brother, Admiral Byng, given by him to Mr. Brough the Marshall a few minutes before his death, March 14, 1757."

ON BOARD HIS MAJESTY'S SHIP MONARQUE,
IN PORTSMOUTH HARBOUR.

A few moments will now deliver me from the virulent Persecution, and frustrate the farther malice of my Enemies—nor need I envy them

a Life subject to the Sensations, my Injuries, and
the Injustice done me must create.   Persuaded I
am, Justice will be done to my reputation here-
after.   The manner and cause of raising and
keeping up the Popular Clamour and Prejudice
against me, will be seen thro'—I shall be con-
sidered (as I now perceive my self) a Victim
destined to divert the Indignation and resentment
of an Injured and deluded people from the proper
Objects—My Enemies themselves, must, even
now, think me Innocent—Happy for me at this
my last Moment, that I know my own Innocence,
and am conscious that no part of my Country's
misfortunes can be owing to me—I heartyly wish
the shedding my Blood may contribute to the
Happyness and Service of my Country—but
cannot resign my just Claim to a faithfull discharge of my Duty, according to the best of my
Judgement, and the utmost exertion of my ability
for His Majesty's Honour, and my Country's
Service—I am sorry that my Endeavours were
not attended with more Success, and that the
Armament under my Command proved too weak
to succeed in an Expedition of such Moment—
Truth has prevailed over Calumny and falsehood,
and Justice has wiped off the ignominious stain of
my supposed want of personal Courage, or
disaffection—My Heart acquits me of these
Crimes—but who can be presumptuously sure of
his own Judgement?—If my Crime is an Error in

Judgement, or differing in oppinion from my
Judges, and if yet, the Error in Judgement
should be on their side—God forgive them, as I
do, and may the Distress of their minds, and
uneasiness of their Consciences, which in Justice
to me they have represented, be relieved, and
subside, as my resentment has done—The
Supreme Judge sees all Hearts, and Motives, and
to Him I must submit the Justice of my Cause.

J. BYNG.

Admiral Byng was fifty-three years old at the time of
his death.   He was buried at Southill, Beds, with this
inscription on his monument :—

To the perpetual disgrace of Publick Justice
The Honble John Byng, Esqre
Admiral of the Fleet
Fell a Martyr to Political Persecution
March 14th in the year 1757, when
Bravery and Loyalty
Were insufficient securities for the
Life and Honour
of a Naval Officer.

There is a small print of Admiral Byng at Chicksands
Priory, at the back of which Mrs. Osborn has inscribed
these words :—

The Honourable John Byng,
Admiral of the Blue,
4th Son of George, Lord Viscount Torrington,
Suffered Political Martyrdom, March 14, 1757,

Whose Memory may this Picture perpetuate,
and at the same time, the depravity of an age
When Publick Justice was prostituted to Private Policy,
And Guilt found protection in the
Blood of the Innocent.   .
When approved Courage and unimpeached Loyalty
confirmed by a forty years faithfull Service,
Were ineffectual Securities for the
Life and Honour
of a British Commander against the
Mistaken resentment of a deluded Populace
and the
Interested Persecution of a State Junto.

———

With this expression of Mrs. Osborn's sentiments on
her brother's unhappy fate, I bring to a close this
terrible page of her life.

1 7 6 6.

———o———

My readers are now asked to carry their minds forward
for a number of years, and to take up the threads of
Mrs. Osborn's history in the year 1766. She herself has
now arrived at the age of seventy-three, and her only
two near relations in the world are her grandsons, Sir
George Osborn and his brother John, to whom her letters
are now addressed. Sir George is occupied with politics
and his regimental duties, and "Jack" has just started
for Naples to be attached to the Embassy there, but not
very happy with his prospects, and complaining that his
uncle, Lord Halifax, had not sufficiently exerted himself
in his interest.

LETTER XLVIII.

[The "Hero of the day" is evidently Mr. Pitt. Conway was Secretary of State, Charles Townshend,
Paymaster of the Forces, Rigby, Secretary to the Duke
of Bedford, Lord Lieutenant of Ireland.]

CHARLES STREET, BERKELEY SQUARE,
January 17, 1766.

My dear Jack,—Since I received your last letter
the day before you was to embarque at Marsielles,
I have not wrote to you. . . . You said we must
not expect to hear from you till February. I am all

impatience for that time, in hopes it may bring a good account of your arrival at Naples, and that you have fixd yourself to your satisfaction there.

I must say you have judgd well not to come home. It is the most severe winter I have felt ever before. Every mortal terible coughs with oppression.

Your brother was all day last Teusday at the House. The man so much adord and feared was the Hero of the day. No one dare speak or reply except his Brother, who he attackd severely—he defyd all Law, set it at nought, blamd the Past and Present, had never conected with any set that had not deceived him, he saw no Ministers there, only men who had got on the Horse of Liberty to ride into places, and then put their Horse in the stable. In short he decryd all sorts and declared his opinion to repeal the Stamp Act, and never to conect with anyone while there remaind so strong an influence from one man. He did not mean to be mistook, did not mean anyone born in England, but on the other side the Tweed. Conway only replyd that he had got on the Horse of Liberty for his Country's service, had been unwillingly drove into place, was ready to turn his horse's head back to the state he was before, yet acknowledgd he would serve with pleasure under him. Sure that was mean ! Charles Townshend had not a word to say, or indeed anyone else. Rigby called for all the Intelligence from America to be printed, which was granted.   They did not know the consequence (young in office indeed!). When they found Bedford lost the same in the other House, they saw their error, and are this day making a strong effort to get that resolution repealed.   This is a specimen of the very disagreable and unstedy situation.   You may communicate to Lord Hillsborough, and then burn it directly. . . . If the Act is repeald, God alone knows the consequence—I tremble.

The match quite fixd with Lady Betty (Montagu) and Lord Hinchingbroke.   Each father gives £1000 a year, your Uncle seems happy to dispose of her to rank and fortune.

The Town is very full, the streets in such a condition coaches are overturned every day; the frost so hard pickaxes cannot mend them.

Lord George Sackville you will see is brought forth again, great murmering about it, none of the Ministers own it their Act, and Mr. Pitt excessively disgusted at that Measure as well as others. . . .

My dear Jack, Adieu. . . . Beauford Ossory and all the young men come home, Wilks too, some say, and some not.

S. O.

LETTER XLIX.

CHARLES STREET, LONDON, *February* 10, 1766.

MY DEAR JACK,—Matters have been in such confusion and uncertainties, indeed little better

now, but next Thursday is hoped will end somthing to purpose, the present Ministry, by George
Byng's intelligence, seem certain to carrie the
point of repeal, the others think different, tis
thought a fortnight more must pass before the
present Agitations can produce change.   King
cannot speak, which is a great misfortune in his
situation . . . honest men cannot be in high
stations without the knowledge necessary to
support themselves, . . . but of whom or what the
next can be composed staggers the wisest among
us . . . and what can spring forth from a time
almost unknown is hard to guess, not a happy face
to be seen. . . .

Lord Halifax has received your letter, and I
hope to have the satisfaction of hearing you are
better, which will bring comfort to your truly
affect.

S. O.

LETTER L.

February 14, 1766.

MY DEAR JACK,—I grieve to find you have been
so much worse than you communicated to me.
We have had the most severe winter with foggs
and all the variety of Bad weather that the
Heavens could pour down upon us.

Tis imposible to paint to you the Horror of
our situation, had you been happy in your wishes,
all must now have vanishd.   Tis inconceivable the

Cloud on every brow, in the present aspect no one in their senses would wish for power.

My dear Jack, I am concernd you sett alone and encourage disagreeable thoughts. I, who am not apt to flatter myself with vain hopes, and false valuations, yet think you have neither lost your time, or have taken any step to reproach yourself . . . every day more and more perplexes, and it must be a bold man who will undertake to set us right. While it rests as it is, you or any friend you have cannot wish you a part in such a dismal whole.

Nothing doing, or can be done in both Houses, but the American affair, in whatever way it is settled will be a millstone about the neck of the present or any future Ministry. Great violence on all sides—very terryfying consequences.

Next Sunday we putt off Black Gloves for Prince Frederick, King of Denmark and Dauphin still to be mourned for.

LETTER LI.

CHARLES STREET, *Feb.* 25, 1766.

MY DEAR JACK,—Your Brother has run away, and left me to ad that the House sitts every day, till $\frac{1}{2}$ hour after ten, but last night till 2 this morning. I think there must be a fresh sett soon, for these will all be demolished. A sad, very sad situation indeed we are in. We have gone on

week after week, and lately have thought every
new day would produce new events, but I see no
end to our distresses. When this Bill is finished,
there must be settled plan to affaires, but God
knows how the scail will turn, those in and those
out equally unhappy, nor do I see any one
prospect to be better. . . .

Mr. Fox was certainly refused (whatever was
thought abroad) when he made his last proposal
here to Miss Greville. She could not bring herself to consent, and therefore he told his friend
Crew she was the woman to make him happy.
He followed his advice and proposed immediatly,
was accepted, and the conclusion to be directly,
to the amazement of the town that one so much
in love as Fox was, should not only resign, but
give her to another. She, however, is a lucky
girl, and the Envy of all the young Women in
town.

Lord and Lady Torrington come to Whitehall
for the winter. She is a very agreeable, sensible
woman, and I think will make him happy.

I can only ad your Brother's affections to those
of, my dear Jack, your truly affect.

Gra. and faithfull Servant.

In conversation at Bushey, I find my Lord has
set his seal upon Ireland. His, I doubt, has been
an unfortunate step that he will repent, he is,
I find, much blamd.

LETTER LII.

14 *March* 1766.

MY DEAR JACK,—Your brother . . . has acquainted you with our political wrangles. The Repeal has gone in the Commons, and in the Lords by a majority of 12. However, the 3rd Reading of the Bill is to be next Monday, when fresh arguments are to be brought, and very many Lords intend to protest. Your Uncle will be of that number. When that is over, 'tis said there will be some Changes. Pitt to take the lead to quiet the Nation, and bring good out of evil if posible. . . .

Last Saturday Lady Betty Montagu was married at her father's house by Dr. Crane. The company were the two fathers, Lady Caroline and Mr. Seymour, half-brother to Lord Sandwich, which with Mr. Melvil and myself were the whole. After the ceremony we had a fine Breakfast, and in half an hour, Lord Hinchingbrook lead his lady into an extreme neat genteel Post Chaise, with four exceedingly pretty bright bay horses, which gallopd all the way to Bushy. Then Lord Sandwich lead me into Lord Halifax's post coach, and followd himself, with poor Melvil hopping after, and Lord Halifax completed the sett. We followd almost in Gallop too, and were at Bushy in an hour and half, where young Montagu came from Eton to meet us. We all stayd there till Monday morning, when the two Lords hastend to their Debates, and I to rest in my own house, after two long days heartily tyerd. We left Bride and Bridegroom there with Melvil, they were to come up tomorrow to their house in Audley Street, but your uncle Lumley dying this morning prevents that, as it will not be propper they should be presented till he is burried.

Lord Scarborough and Lord Halifax met this evening to open the will . . . the town says Lumley to Lord Scarborough, with the house in town, and great mortgages on both. Stansted to Lord Halifax, coal mines, etc., to the value of £100,000, great mortgages also on them.

Mr. Crew and Miss Grevil, Duke of Beauford and Miss Boscawen, Lord Strathmore and Miss Bows, were the dancing lovers last night at Almacks. These three Wedings are to be celebrated as soon as the Lawyers can finish.

It seems Beauford was in love with Boscawen before he left England. Dutches Beauford crys night and day. She wanted a woman of fortune and Quality, and had Lady Betty Montagu in her eye, which would have been more discreet, but fate, I hope, designs them all happy with their mates.

y^r truly affec.

S. O.

LETTER LIII.

CHARLES STREET, 15 *April* 1766.

MY DEAR JACK,—The good account you give of yourself both in body and spirits has had the

same good effect on me as the fine Climate you
are in has had on you. Your Brother would have
wrote himself today, but that he is on Guard,
and also nothing materiel is on the anvil at
present. The recess of Parliam^t during the Easter
hollydays has kept the Town empty and quiet,
and not a word of Politics has transpired, only
the grave thinking men look upon them to have
been fatally conducted.

No one is happy as they foresee that without
some miracle we are undone. This week the
Parliament has mett again. Yesterday was entertaining to those not concernd. Strange management that a materiel point was to be the business
of the day, but no Chancellor of the Exchequer
there, or anyone of the Ministry to support it.
Pitt went down to be quite against the Question.
Thomas Townshend and Onslow proposed it.
I think it was an alteration in the Malt Tax. Pit
said he was entirely against these measures, it
struck at the Prorogative of the Crown, and totally
disliked the whole, so much that they knockd
under and said it was not a Measure of Government but a Measure entirely of their own, which
brought a laugh on them and on the Ministry too
to find no head there, and the business to be
carried on at the caprice of anyone who chose to
start up and propose their own schemes. George
Grenville was there, but said not a word, left it
to battle it among themselves, and all the sensible

people laughing in their sleves at such a materiel affair under such management.

Wednesday next a Bugett is to be open, after that more may be said.

The young part of the town thinks of nothing but Wedings.   Duke Beaufort to Miss Boscawen, the Admiral's daughter.   His mother so angry at the match, she would not see them till after the ceremony was over, and then just for them to receive her Blessing, and stepd into their Post Chaise at Badmington.

Mr. Crew was also few days after married to Miss Grevill, they say she refused Fox,—most monstrous are the settlements he has made upon her, and Lady Mary Fitzpatrick has reconciled herself to take her leavings, and next week is to marry Fox.   His father gives them £4000 a year in present, and 10 at his death.   A fine match for her, 'tis a lucky year for the Ladies without fortune.

The suitable match which pleases everybody is Lady Dorothy Cavendish, Duke Devonshire's sister, to the Duke of Portland, but does not take place till August.

Lord Halifax came here next day after he received your letter, . . . he looks well, and is now strong on his own footing.

We have had severall weding dinners, the first at Lord Guilford's, where were the 3 Earls and there 3 Eldest sons.   Ld Guilford, Ld North,

Ld Sandwich (Ld Hinchingbrook not well, could not be there), therefore Ld Sandwich youngest son, George Montagu, your Brother, and myself, tomorow the same company at Lady Betty Archers.

I have hardly left room to ad your brother's affections with those, my dear Jack,

of your most truly affec.

Gra^{mr}.

LETTER LIV.

April 29, 1766.

MY DEAR JACK,—I begin this large sheet in hopes your Brother will fill it with more materiel subjects than my pen can afford, since even common Chatt deserts my House, now the charms of Ranelagh engages her votarys, and hurrys all other amusements to give that a place in their time. The ladies at least will have reason to approve the way of life they are in, since all the matches are in their favor. Beauty overbalances cash, and all future considerations. Miss Bisshopp is the next, to a Mr. Dummer, a great Estate and fine seat in Hampshire. . . .

An ugly report creeps about that Mr. Hervey and another English gentleman are lost by their curiosity leading them to Mont Vesuvius just as the Eruption broke out, if so, you know it, therefore no more on that subject.

Tis said the House will be up at Whitsuntide.

Pitt is quite a Harlequin, one day appears in one shape, the next quite contrary, roasts all sides, says there is not an honest man to councel with, therefore will stand alone. The mongrel curs of the present times, shrink and creep, and fall down at his footstool, watch his nod, and would shew implicit obedience to his will, but he does as all great minds should do,—dispise sycophants.

The Division grown stronger, but what will come of it none can tell. Your cousin George Byng is so angry they will not go through thick and thin with one another that he almost resolves never to come in Parliament again. . . . I see nothing yet but doubt and dispair, when the sun will shine again I know not, the Learned say there is a spot on the sun biger than this world, which perhaps is the reason of so many clouded understandings. This and the large Comet employ the curious at Flamsteds, Greenwich Park. Your friend Lord Forbes when he left you at Brussels, went to one of the French provinces to learn the language, which he did to such perfection that he spent £8000 when he came to Paris, and there fell in love with Lady Georgina Berkeley. He is now in England in your Brothers Regiment, and she came over lately, and they renewd their former conversations, . . . and she is now Lady Forbes. His father so angry at this destructive match and his Paris extravagance, he vows to set him aside and give his Estate to his grandson.

Your brother is now busie with field days, but has charged me with his best affections to you, you are always sure those of yours sincerely,

S. O.

I believe few post days for 50 years past have escaped from my hand in the Post Office, so that I imagine it so well known there I can never disguise.

LETTER LV.

13 *May* 1766.

MY DEAR JACK,—I am extremely disappointed that no letter from you is come . . . the very great distance between us is an unpleasant circumstance, but I will not inlarge on that subject, only hope it will establish your Health.   Tis as endless as uncertain to send you accounts of the situation of the present times, which varies every day. The Parliament setts till ten or twelve most nights.   The mountain only produces a mouse, for all seems at a stand, nothing done, nothing pleasing to anyone.

Duke Grafton has certainly given warning, but is desired to remain till they can provide themselves with one to supply his place.   I am weary and so is everybody at these uncertainties. Every creature is going out of town, more particularly all the men of business.   It seems as if everything was left to be governd by Chance and haphazard, and yet Parliamᵗ will not be up till June.

Torrington gone to find an agreeable hunting seat in Lincolnshire. Halifax settling his own affaires, has full employment in doing that. I hope he will retrieve his losses, and satisfy all concernd in them, and be a free man before he retakes those of a higher nature, for certainly sooner or later he will have office again.

I dont intend stiring out of town, but wait and watch for the pleasure of hearing from you,

being most affectionately yours—

LETTER LVI.

[The Lally here alluded to was a French officer, Governor of Pondicherry, which he surrendered to the English, and was beheaded in France 1766. The circumstances of the case had some similarity with those of Admiral Byng's conviction.]

CHARLES STREET, *May* 30, 1766.

MY DEAR JACK,—This being my turn, I take it to say that however your mind is discomposed with your present situation, your Brother and I bear an equal share with you, but we all three must make use of the senses and reason God has given us, and not sink under the unavoidable state of our present circumstances. While I live, which in all human probability cannot be long, you shall be supported, so make yourself easy.

Duke Grafton is gone out without being able to serve his father-in-law, though greatly desirous to do it. Duke of Richmond is come in, more unfit than any, so that things grow worse and worse. Lord North has refused one of the Vice Treasureships of Ireland, and none that have a grain of Understanding will take any concerns upon them, no, not the Ministers abroad. The other day Torrington asked a principal, Who was to go to such a Court? He answered, You, if you please, for we dont find those we wish for will accept. In short, I must give you this comfort that tis a much greater disgrace to be in than out. The Parliament not yet up. They get together forty members, and pass what Bills they please, no one knows or cares, even the members who are in town dont care to attend, such a time I never remember.

No account has yet come of Lord Charles Montagu and his fine wife being landed at his Government of North Carolina. While they livd in St. James' Palace before they went, they livd well, had their dinner and wine from Thatched House, the bill for four months was £1200.

You give us no account of Mont Vesuvius, tho' this Erruption is often seen at Naples, . . . pray give us news of this extraordinary matter.

Dont laugh when I tell you there has been one of our men of war sent from a part in the East Indies in search of an Island which they had the

fortune to find, and landed some of the crew to
discover the sort of people upon it.   They found
them a strong robust people 8 f' and half high.
A girl of thirteen was 7 feet, and others in
proportion.   They were cloathed with skins of
Beasts, invited our people to go farther up the
Country, but they were satisfied with the dis-
covery, and returned.   Part of this was in our
newspapers.   I concluded it a Guliver Island,
and that it was a Joke, but at Admiral Osborns
last night they confirmed the truth, and therefore
I conclude it is so.

Lallys fate is compared to my poor brother's,
two innocent men sacrificed to Ministers purposes.
In an article from France, I see the comparison,
and before that from private conversation.

Your Brothers sincere affections are ever joynd
with mine to you.

LETTER LVII.

July 1st, 1766.

MY DEAR JACK,—I set down to write to you
with a mind as gloomy as the weather, which has
been continualy weeping for ten weeks past.   The
thundering and lightening we have lately had has
made me hope it would clear the clouds, and let
us once more see the sun, however these hopes are
vain, and weeping still continues, to the sorrow of
those who have large crops of Hay all spoiling.

I must begin with the maloncholy tale of your

Aunt Jekyll's death. . . . I cannot think what can become of her daughter, poor girl, to whom she is an irreparable loss, to poor Miss Roberts, her companion also, though she livd like a toad under a Harrow.   Lord Halifax was then at Horton, . . . but he went and stayd with her till she dyed . . . you must mourn 3 week, black sword and buckels, 3 weeks coloured ones with your mourning coat . . . her violent temper was a misfortune, but who is without fault? Your brother is with Lord Halifax at Horton, returns next week to Chicksands. . . .

My dear Jack, what is it posible for us to do for you, when you consider the impropriety of a man in opposition asking a favor . . . if you were here opertunitys might offer and you would be known to people who could serve you, they will not take a man in the clouds they know nothing off.   Everyone knows, and the King too, why you quitted Brussels . . . when you can be served you certainly will, but while you are absent believe me, nothing can be done for you.

Lord Halifax can do nothing, Lord North refuses all offers made him, none of the Outs think they can with honour accept, much less ask for any favors.   So many things are vacant, and no acceptors: Treasury, Navy vacant, Vice-treasureship of Ireland, with several other things that is amazing goes begging.

I am your truly affect.

LETTER LVIII.

July 4, 1766.

MY DEAR JACK,—Though I wrote a long letter last Tuesday, I set down to a fresh sheet of paper today. There is no one appointed to Viena yet—no scheme subsists twenty-four hours. . . . I don't wonder you have no notion of these things, because it is entirely new. I have before told you of great offers to those who I hope will serve you, but he will not accept, sees it is with a halter round his neck.

His nephew North they would buy at any rate, but he will not be an apostate. How long this confused state of affairs may last no one can tell. Providence has often brought us from the brink of ruin, I therefore trust we shall still be saved.

Let me intreat you to turn your thoughts home . . . you can live in credit like a gentleman on £320 or £340 a year. . . . By the time this reaches you, you will be 23, not an age to be very miserable, though Fortune has been a Gilt.

y' truly affect.

S. O.

LETTER LIX.

[The person mentioned by Sarah whose picture is at Chicksands, is certainly Oliver Cromwell. There is a portrait of him by Lely there.]

Fryday, 18 *July* 1766.

MY DEAR JACK,—The very next post after I wrote, I could have told you the bustle was beginning, and things come in earnest to a crisis. The wheels so clogd, Government was at a stop and pulled up dead short. The King sent for Pit, and Pit is come, and most certain has a carte blanche, on no other terms would he undertake, so he gets himself master of the position. Was heated with his journey, but saw the King next day, which was this day was senight. All is conjecture, the only certain thing is that Pitt comes in, but in what place is not yet settled, only that he will carve for himself, and make up a Ministry of those who will be guided by him. . . .

Mr. Pit and Lord Temple have mett, but so far from agreeing, they were very warm, and Mr. Pitt so ruffled by it that he has forbid anyone to come to him on business for two days, for his fever is much encreasd. How will he bear the ruffles of the whole kingdom on his shoulders?
. . . But I own I am glad he is to be Prime Minister, twill quiet the nation and cool the minds of all dissatisfied, as well as strike terror abroad, where I doubt in our present situation we must be dispised. Tis said the Citty intend to go in a body to thank the King the day after Pitt is appointed. Are you not stagard to find Prince Ferdinand has resignd all his employments to King of Prussia, and tis affirmd has accepted of all Marshall Saxe's appointments in France? I dare not trust on paper what is said on that event here. In short, we talk much of the times

when the person governd whose picture is over one of the doors of the blue room at Chicksands.

Your uncle (Ld Hal.) just stepd in here, said . . . he will asist you all in his power, in any thing but a direct request to the Ministry. . . .

I must now tell you a little chat. . . . Lady Montrath is dead, has left Lord John Cavendish £40,000, never saw him but once in her life, only because he was a Patriot, and some more Patriot legacies to people she did not know.   She was a Bradford, and maddish, and so she has lived and dyed, her son is the same, therefore all her riches of no value.

Pit has the reversion of Lady Grandisons £9000 a year, if young Villiers her son dyes under age.   He is inclynd to be wild, and has not had the small pox, and Pit is lucky.   There- fore everyone concludes the Boy is to dye.   Lord Wm Campbell was appointed to the Government of Nova Scotia in the room of your cousin, Colonel Wilmot.

Adieu, my dear Jack,
believe me affectionately yours.

LETTER LX.

August 1st, 1766.

MY DEAR JACK,—I must acquaint you last Wednesday kissd hands :

Pitt now Earl of Chatham—Lord Privy Seal.

Lord Northington—Lord President.

Lord Campden—Lord Chancellor.

Lord Shelburn—S. of State.

Conway remains the other.

Duke of Grafton — 1st L^d of the Treasury.

Charles Townshend—Chancell^r of the Excheq^r.

Mr. Stanly—Ambassador to Russia.

Mr. Campbell—A Lord of Treasury.

The above are certain—Dowdeswell is to be provided for, some say Speaker, some say Joint Paymaster with James Grenville. . . . Ld Dartmouth has resignd, is Lord of Trade, Duke of Newcastle has refused a pention of £4000 a year. People are not pleased. Pit will loose popularity by loosing his name. Sir James Porter went to Lord Chatham, Duke of Grafton, to make his ceremonial visits to them, none at home . . .

believe me ever affectionately yours.

LETTER LXI.

12 *August* 1766.

MY DEAR JACK,—I am much distressd what to say in this letter, since tho a change is accomplished, we are no better, no longer Pitt but Earl of Chatham, this was the fall of the popular Poultney when Earl of Bath. All the joy and expectations of our great Patriots and indeed the whole nation, seems quite damp, for he has not taken the leading place, is only Privy Seal, and now out of the House of Commons, where all the Business must lye.   However he has made Charles Townshend Chancellor Excheq^r, who is to lead, and who has undoubted abillities, but there you must stop.   It is understood that Chatham is to guide the whole, and be absolutely supream.   The manner as well as the fact of discarding those turnd out of the late Ministry has disoblidged them, Rockingham extremely so. Our old friends go by the title of Bedford faction. Pitt and Temple quite at variance, pamphlets, epigrams, odes, and more witt flying about than for some years past. . . . Letters are wrote that the King wants men of abillities, and those who are possessed of them are expected to serve him in the capacities they are most able for.   Ld Granby Commander in Chief of the Army.   Stanly goes to Russia, Ellis to Spain, he was very far from a friend to your Uncle.

Your brother came to London to mount guard on Sunday.   I am sure his fortune cannot support opposition to Ongley, but he acts by Lord Halifax's advice. . . . Many talk of resigning, many they want to do so, but won't it is recond, I know not if true.   Quite a Bureau affair.   Can it be possible such oyl and vinegar could incorporate?   Tis said and by Pamphlets provd, Bute and Pitt are so. Some think this cannot hold. Poor England, what will become of her?

LETTER LXII.

15 *August* 1766.

MY DEAR JACK,—Except you was on the spot, you can form no idea of our fluctuating situation, the like I believe, is without example since the time of Charles I. Mr. Pitt, who was the idol, and by whose influence so many favoured schemes were applauded last winter, by only his name to give them sanction, is now tore to pieces by all sides, that name is sunk, and they are violent against L⁴ Chatham, his friends aghast, his foes triumphant. You never answer, if our news-papers and Pamphlets are ever seen at Naples.

Things are far from settled yet. Duke Grafton 1st L⁴ Treasurer. Shelburn and Conway Secretaries of State—since these are fixd there are resignations and dismissions every day. John York and Charles Saunders resignd Admiralty last week, and this week L⁴ Egmont, so there hardly a Board for bussiness. . . . All this instability is very unfortunate for Government. I can only add that if Mr. Pitt can surmount the prejudices taken against Lord Chatham, and be steady in his guidance, which is absolutely fixd in himself alone, and be more than human by blunting all his feelings to this Clamor against him,

things may by his perseverance stand on former
ground,—but if not, things will grow too powerfull for any guidance, and throw us into I know
not what, nor dare I think of a name for it.   I am
in hopes he will lay aside prejudice of party feuds,
by taking in those of the best abillitys on all
sides. . . . All people displeasd, don't trust the
Cabinet. . . . *August* 19.—We are a strange
disconcerted people — no one cares to accept
Admiralty.

LETTER LXIII.

CHARLES STREET, *Fryday, September* 5, 1766.

I here inclose the Ode you desired me, by Mrs.
Greville, but I hope you won't implore Oberon,
for Pope says the Passions are the Elements of
Life, without them the blood would stagnate.
Sherbet is the beverage of mortals, and to omit
anyone of the ingredients would render it insipid
and tasteless.   Sir George Pocock is varstly
unhinged at his wife's illness, he sees and knows
her danger, but must keep up spirits with her.
What avails all the treasures of the East and
West Indies pourd into their laps, it will bring no
happyness. . . .

Everything in this country without stabillity,
no one at present so happy in it as Lord Bristol
and Hervey.   If I have any judgment, next
winter will be a crisis.   I saw Lord Stormont

yesterday, he goes to Viena next month. The clamours are as much against Pitt as they were in regard to Predecessors, and yet I hope he will hold it. Fifteen Admirals was disoblidged at Saunders being put at the head of the Admiralty, tis thought can only mean a step for Keppel to rise into that seat, in short disobligations are numerous, and consequently clamours. Ld Bristol is appointed to Ireland, and is to reside there constantly. The King desired to appoint the Secretary, whom he told him was his brother Augustus—£3000 a year.

Lord Hertford is Master of the Horse. Duke of Rutland satisfyed with Lord Granby being Commander in Chief,—tis in vain to send you a red book, unless one was printed every month.

I am in hopes you will come back with Sir George Pocock, but this is man's appointment, God may disappoint the whole.

LETTER LXIV.

LONDON, 17 *September* 1766.

MY DEAR JACK,—Everything continues amazingly uncertain, I dont think Townshend or North will continue. God knows when our cards will be trumps again, . . . they talk of the Bedford partie coming in. Lord Weymouth Cofferer insted of Lord Scarborough. Parliament certainly is to meet beginning of November, the Proclamation

is already out for its doing so.   Sir George
Pocock thinks himself ill-used, . . . before he set
out for Naples, he kissd hands on leave, and then
had an Audience, and expressd his Resentment
at having had no reward for 45 years services,
had been promised a Peerage, and even that
forgot. . . .

Sir Thomas Alston intends to declare for our
County, and as he is very flighty, imposible he
can make anything of it, yet I think it will put
your Brother in a cleft stick.   Lord Barrymore
next month when he is of age to marry Lady
Amelia Stanhope, Lord Harrington's 3rd daughter.
Lord Mont Steward not yet marryd to Miss
Windsor.   6 October Admiral Keppel is to convoy our Princess Caroline, the Queen of Denmark,
to the Hague, from thence she is to have a
miserable journey through Westphalia and cross
the sea to Denmark.

Letter lxv.

Teusday, 23 *Sept*ʳ 1766.

MY DEAR JACK,—Believe me you cannot judge
of affaires at the distance you are from us, . . . it
has really given me infinite disquiet to find you
fix your mind from Castles in the air, . . . was
you here, you would see things in a different
light, the Systym of Government, families and
connections are all moved by new springs   . .

if you knew the squables and dificultys they had to strugle with in the times that you think so hardly on, when they felt the ground they stood on was a bog, you would not judge as you do.

I have enquired how to get the Protest. I find a Peer may ask a copy, but as none are in town that I know, it will not be posible yet a while. There is a rumour as if some sort of Coalition would take place before the Parliament meet in November, they talk of Lord Gower, Rigby and Lord Weymouth, who are all the Bedford friends. This will be a curious winter, for though I am 73, I have never seen anything like it.

Lord and Lady Hinchingbrook dind with me yesterday. All your relations are married, and will have children and grandchildren before you come home. I shall wish to live till May, that I may once more see you, being, my dear Jack, most affectionately yours.

LETTER LXVI.

LONDON, *Oct.* 7, 1766.

MY DEAR JACK, — Being Chargé D'Affaires is the most desirable thing in your situation, and will give you credit and reputation to have been so at two Courts.

I fear I have seemd to write a little cross in my two or three last letters; if I did so it was occasioned by your writing your intermediate thoughts. . . .

Several are drawing off, profess they will link to no party. The Borough of Oxford is given to Lord Hertford for his services in London. This is an unprecedented note above a pention, for it is for ever. Lord Northumberland is made a Duke. No happy faces anywhere. It used to be, those out pout, and those in grin, but out or in all is pout, . . . we must be the redicule of all foreign Courts.

Our Princess Matilda was married by Proxie last Wednesday, and Thursday morning set out for Harwich and so in the Yatch to Hollond, and so to her King at Copenhagen. The Queen is happy with her Princess Royal. Prince Henry is created Duke of Cumberland.

Lord Halifax to shoot, and enjoy the sweets of the life of a country gentleman. Since I wrote my other sheet, I must inform you Sir James Gray is appointed for Spain, and Lord Cardross, Lord Buchan's eldest son, is appointed Secretary to the Embassie, therefore all that view is lost.

Your truly affectionate Gra.

LETTER LXVII.

14 *October* 1766.

MY DEAR JACK,—Had you been here posibly we might have got you to Paris a Volunteer with Lord Rochford. . . . Lord Grantham has given

up the Post Office, they talk of Rigby for it.
I suppose that is to sooth the Bedford party.
Marquis's in number to be made. Lord Chatham
is now our whole Governor, I wish he may work
mericles, but all this placing and displacing shews,
I think, a timidity. There is no partie, everything is blended together, no connections, for they
tye and untye every day as convenience and advantage offer. Honor and faith and friendship may
be scratchd out of the Dictionary, for they are all
words without meanings, in short, my dear Jack,
I will not think, for tis in vain. Everything here
is persueing a shadow, all is delusion. I hope,
however, that I shall keep an old fashion heart,
and remain most truly your affectionate.

LETTER LXVIII.

28 *October* 1766.

MY DEAR JACK,—I sent your last letter to your
brother at Chicksands, but he is rambling about
to Newnham and Greatworth, and Lord Halifax
is rambling too. There can be no expectation of
anything this winter by his interest. Petitions,
peerages, places are lavishly given, all to prevent
the Rockingham and Bedford joyning, they will
be powerfull indeed if it cannot be prevented, and
the present conductors must be overturned. Be
carefull and cautious of the Hollonds and Foxes,
and dont let a word transpire to them of what

your letters say.   Caution Hamilton also.   Duke
of Buccleughs brother is dead of a fever at Paris,
greatly lamented, they say much superior to his
brother.   You knew him.

This day fortnight Parliament is to meet.

No mortal yet come to town.

Nov 4th. . . . Your Sir James Porter has had
all his family inoculated, and all is well and over.
Mr. Villiers, L^d. Grandison's son, was inoculated
from the subject taken from them, but not yet
come out. . . .

The month of May will I hope, turn all things
to suit the pleasures that spring should produce.
One year goeth and another cometh, with every
change to hurt, not only individuals, but the
whole.

We have a very uncomfortable prospect, the
poor murmuring and rising in all parts, provisions
at so exorbitant a rate, they must starve except
the Parliament can find means to prevent Fore-
stallers who monopolize all things that ought to
have been in common to the people.   Your
Brother has only had power to make his tenants
cry, but not to make them sell their grain at a
reasonable price.   They keep their barns full, in
hopes by the scarcity to sell it at an immoderate
rate, and indeed they deserve it.   The Mob, or
by what other name they will be calld, will level
all to the ground, and there will be neither Barns
or grain left — they have been very desperate

in many countrys, and have reason, tho these riotous proceedings must be suppressd if posible. Liberty is gone to too great a length.   Adieu.

LETTER LXIX.

5 December 1766.

MY DEAR JACK,—We have moved every spring we could for you. . . . I got a proper friend to recommend you to our great Commander in the shape of Admiral Byng's nephew. . . . Lord Ossory is chiefly where hunting and horses can be his devertion, does not seem to care to be a Senator yet.   I fancy his turn is not very agreeable to his uncle. . . . Our two new brides, Dutches Portland and Lady Montstewart, have exceeding brilliant equipages, the whole conversation is at present on that subject.   They were both presented at Court last week.   White Coaches, or rather a petit Gris colour, silk reines and topings cut a most glaring and spreaded appearance.   The ladies may look happy, but I see no man that looks so.

Tis feard General Stenwix and his family are lost coming from Ireland a month since, and have not been heard of.

Wether Prerogative, Liberty, or Aristocracy is to be the thing this winter who can tell.   Some shape surely must be found.   If I had no children, I should not care a fig, but as it is otherways I am not so easy.

No time or reign has ever produced events like the present.   Surely some malignant star influences our conduct.   All is Helter Schelter, sense and reason is fled to other climes.   Keppel not only resignd Admiralty, but Bedchamber, . . . on this break the Bedfords were sought.   The Duke said he would come up and negotiate himself, would not transact through seconds, but before he arrived, Sir Edward Hawk, Sir Percy Bret and Jenkinson were appointed to the Admiralty.   He thought this so great a slight, he broke all off, and returnd to Woburn, and will I conclude be bitterer than ever.   Delawar Master Horse — everyone gapeing for this extraordinary place. Tell Sir George Pocock of all these outs and ins, but be cautious, no one knows Who is Who. This day to be a great one (5 Dec^r) in the House of Commons.   Your Brother will write next post.   Tis in regard to the dispensing power, an exact pararel to the General Warrants, only they change sides. . . .

Believe me, dear Jack, in all your situations, I shall be most faithfully yours.

LETTER LXX.

CHARLES STREET, BERKELEY SQUARE,
January 2nd, 1767.

MY DEAR JACK,—My best wishes have, I hope, reached you in time for the New Year, and I repeat them again. Severall mournings also present themselves to you, not only your Aunt Margaret Osborn, but poor Lady Guilford; you must mourn for six weeks. Commissioner Osborn also is in grief for his only son George, he was a puny boy, and not like to have spirit for this world, but a Parent feells the affliction, and cannot alleviate by such reflections. Whenever you return you will find Death has made a sweep among your family and friends. The Commissioner and Admiral are very tottering, and seem almost ready to obey his call. I say nothing of one more near.

Lady Guilford has disappointed many expectations by making her will entirely in Lord Guilford's favour. Lord Bolingbroke choosing to spend all at Arthur's and Newmarket was no essential loss to him, since all would have gone there, and being parted from his wife, no prospect of his children proving better than their parents. . . . The Estate was recond £4000 a year, this is lucky for Lord North. . . . Lord Cornwallis is made Justice in Eyre, £2000 a year. He is with his Reg*. at Minorca, the last letter from him said he intended to spend Carnival in Italie, and not come home till spring, but this employ is given to him unsolicited. . . . Every step of these times are astonishing, seems as if caprice had a share . . . at present hope is all we live on. Adieu.

LETTER LXXI.

CHARLES STREET, 13 *January* 1676.

MY DEAR JACK,—It is an uncommon expression of affection to say I rejoyce at your being at Naples, for England this winter is Moscovy, so severe a climate has not been here since the year 1740. Intense cold and snow so deep no communication of roads, that even the post is day beyond the usal time, and the streets in London almost impassable. What must poor wretches suffer who can have neither Victuals, Cloaths, or Work to procure them any, when even those who enjoy the blessing of comforts, so hardly endure it.

The turn of times here is too unaccountable to be credited . . . at present both England and Ireland are under Chatham's thumb, a secret spring may guide the motions, but the ways are unsearchable, and past finding out.

Lord Bristol says publickly he shall not move in Ireland but under the direction of Lord Chatham.

Lord Barrymore's day was fixd for Lady Amelia Stanhope, the dinner prepard at Lord Harrington's, the Bride dressd, when behold the messenger with letter acquainted him Lord Barrymore was taken ill, and his Physician advised him to put off the Weding, he has been ill ever since, some believe it, others don't, and think he repents.

Your Uncle Lord Halifax is in grief, has lost his only son George.

My dear Jack, may health and prosperity attend you.

                  -    your truly affect.

LETTER LXXII.

Teusday, February 10, 1767.

MY DEAR JACK,—It is just a month since I wrote to you, when I was taken ill in the midle of writing that letter, however I finished it in my bed before the post went out.   From that time I had Sir Clifton Wintringham seventeen days twice a day.   I have still relapses, but while Bleeding relieves, here I shall be.   At 73 how long, God alone knows.   Your brother was sent for and came all night in that dreadfull snow. . . . I am perfectly resignd to the Will of Heaven, for I consider myself of no use to either of you. . . .

Feb. 20.—I hear Miss Bows is married this day to Lord Strathmore.   The two brides who make the principal conversation at present are Mr. George Pitt's daughter, bred in convent at Sens, from which Mr. Legonier fetchd her.   At present her dress is the wonder of the town, her head a yard high, and filld or rather coverd with feathers to an enormous size, fitter for a Masquerade than a drawingroom.   The other is Lady Guidon, who was Miss Wilmot, her headdress is as high, but is built up like a rock with diamonds, and indeed she is so much coverd with jewels, that they compare her to a lark wrapped up in crumbs. Lord Chatham is again detain at Marlborow, the whole machin of government therefore stands still. Parliament meets on pretence of business, but postpones it to a future day.

Your brother desires me to say he will write as soon as our great Director comes to put the wheels in motion. At present there is no spirit but what newspapers spit forth, for things are grown too serious to bear a joke. I may totter on for some time, tho alterd in person yet never can in my affection for you, while I crawl on this earth and am able to tell you so. Adieu.

LETTER LXXIII.

LONDON, *March* 6, 1767.

MY DEAR JACK,—I can now assure you I am better, though I must not expect a return of strength at my time of day that cannot be recruited. Lord Halifax, his son and daughter dined here last Saterday, but I was not able to go down to dinner. The Ministry lost the question by 18 last fryday, and they did not endeavour to battle it or devide the House on the report next day. Most people are pleasd that 3d Land Tax is gained by the Opposition. Lord North from being in office must use his brightest talents,

L

but was left in the lurch by Lord Charles
Townshend, whom he was to support, and who
soon gave up the point himself. Shelburn was
dispatchd next morning to Marlborough, where
our principal and indeed *sole guide* has been laid
up with the gout at an inn, twas said so bad, he
could neither return or come forward, but Shel-
burne's intelligence of defeat electrified him, and
into his coach he got imediatly, away to London,
and to the King, and tis now said a defeat is of
no consequence, and that tis all right.   New ways
of thinking transpire every day.

Duke of Buccleugh is very soon to marry Lady
Betty Montagu's daughter.   Lady Dalkeith, his
mother, so happy with the match she could not
sleep for three nights after it was settled.   Last
Saturday Hariot Bladen was married to Lord
Essex.   Poor Lady Amelia Stanhope must see
many more matches concluded before her own,
for Lord Barrymore is oblidged to submit to a
salivation, which he is now in, before he can be
a bridegroom.   Almacks, Soho, Concerts, Bur-
lettas and Operas engages all the idle people every
night, which makes such invalids as myself much
alone.   Parties at cards and assemblies take all
their turn, so that the hours and days are much
too short for all that must be done, and we are
now in the hight of our diversions.

My dear Jack, I am yours with very tender
affection.   Adieu.

LETTER LXXIV.

March 17, 1767, LONDON.

MY DEAR JACK,—By this time I conclude it is time to find you at Rome. . . . There is nothing here but confusion, every department a rope of sand. I believe History does not afford the like, every partie, every connection broke to peices. Sir James Grey not gone yet. He laboured much against any Secretary to the Embassy being appointed, said they were of no use and that it would be a great saving to Government to strike off that expence, they have not reguarded his Occonomy, and today I hear a younger brother of Lord Walpole's is to be appointed . . . here is almost Lady Day and nothing done, all the Chiefs have their several convenient maladies, one or two the gout, that by one impediment or other all bussiness is posponed, no Budget yet opend, no plan of Supply. One day Charles Townshend was on the point to resign, he had slunk away into the Citty and could not be found, but no one would accept his place, therefore all met again, shook hands and friends, all this must appear to you to be children's play.

Lord Tavistock's accident is a miserable affair. This day senight at the Redborn Hunt of near 50 gentlemen, his horse in a leap came too short over and fell, throwd Lord Tavistock off, who catching at bridle, made the horse plunge, and struck both stomach and head, and fracturd his scul. He was taken up speachless, and carried to a farm House where he still is, his life or death yet uncertain. Gataker was sent immediatly. The horse had trapand him, and therefore Gataker had only to take out the splinterd bones and peices of scul. The chance is yet against him, as you may guess from the situation he is in, somtimes favourable accounts, at other dispairing ones. There is a large afflicted family, and indeed the whole town lamenting the unfortunate case. There are two sons, but what a blow to the tender passions of his parents and wife, as well as the Pride and ambition of his father, and indeed a loss to our county.

Your brother's love attends you, with that of your truly affect. Gra.

Letter LXXV.

Teusday, 22 March 1767.

My dear Jack,—Tho' they began polling at Northampton last Thursday, yet there is not a probability of it being over under 4 or 5 days. Therefore postpone all things relating to that expensive and troublesome affair till the end of this letter, in hopes there may be a final determination of it before I seal it. . . . We are now in the midst of faction and riot. Wilkes has daringly stepd forth with an audacious attempt to stand for the Citty, and tho he is an Outlaw, bids defiance to Government. . . . I hope he has no chance of being chose a Citty member, tho' yesterday a coach with six horses was ready to take him off the hustings to the place of dinner, and when half way they took out the horses, and carryd his Coach themselves, strange infatuation! but all this is Mob. . . . Tis said 2 millions will be spent in Elections, £20 and £30,000 comes out of every purse. Nabobs, Contractors, Silversmiths, bankrupts, are in high luck, there will hardly be 200 real gentlemen in the House. The landed Interest dyed with the last Parliament. . . . Adieu, affect. yours.

LETTER LXXVI.

CHARLES STREET, BERKELEY SQUARE,

Teusday, 24 *March* 1767.

MY DEAR JACK, — My last wrote to you this day senight to Rome had the Particuler and dismal account of poor Lord Tavistock's accident. By that you could entertain no hope of a favourable one in my next, therefore not surprised when I tell you he languished under many severe operations till yesterday morning, when at 4 oclock he dyed. The faculty never had the least hope of his recovery, tho' gave flattering ones to the Duke of Bedford, and therefore the thunderbolt has almost demolished him. You know his passions are strong, and he is almost distracted. Poor Lady Tavistock who never was permitted to see him, tho' went to a house within a quarter of a mile where he lay, but the agitation of seeing her was not to be venturd,—she was brought to town yesterday neither dead nor alive, has been in fitts ever since, and greatly to be pittyd, for they were very happy. She has two boys, and in time I hope will take comfort in them as I have done in mine. My loss was a Tavistock to me, and therefore I feel greatly for the whole family.

Your brother by advice of his friends has wrote circular letters, it was agreed by all that he stood pledgd to the County by his applycation last summer, and therefore his offer now could not be avoided, . . . there must immediatly be a meeting appointed, and he must then judge his strength. Lord Tavistock is an irreparable loss to our County, there will not be a proper head to it left when Duke Bedford dyes, this must shorten his days, and damp all ambitions, he is now extremly ill. You cannot conceive how all people from the King to the labourers lament for Lord Tavistock, there never was greater grief. Ossory is so shy in the country that no one there takes to him, but how far the tenderness of people's Hearts may move them to indulge the Duke of Bedford in the person of his nephew, a little time will shew otherways.   Alston who has great interest intends going down to the Meeting and supports y^r Brother with all his power. T'will appear a bold stroke for a private gentleman, to bring an opposition against so powerfull a person, and two such powerfull purses, it sounds running his head against a brick wall.   Pray God send him well out of this scrape.

LETTER LXXVII.

LONDON, 31 *March* 1767.

MY DEAR JACK,—I fret a little to find after next quarter y^r income will decrease, since I conclude you will think it right to resign your studentship by that time. . . . This has been a trying winter for old and young.   Death has made great havock and caused much grief in many families, that of the Bedfords exceeds all the rest.

Lady Cork has such continual histerick fitts that it has shewd the shocking effects on the poor Dungarvan who is quite an idiot.   Duke of Manchester must seek another country, the house in this square to be sold, the castle in the country to be let, but who is there can take it ?   He has not paid a tradesman since his father dyed.

At present I am wore down, lye upon the first flour, not able to go up or down.   We have a long severe winter which continues still, tho tomorrow is April.   The chance is against me, 70 od weighs very heavy in the scail, but whenever it happens I shall dye in the assurance that you two Brothers will preserve an inviolable friendship for each other as long as you live.

The Hinchinbrookes say they cannot live on £2000 a year rent charge, which is as good as £2500 Estate, they talk of retireing into the Country. There surely is some Influence over this Island, no one is happy or settled, . . . your brother is gone into Beds. to try his strength at the election. I think he has no chance, for all the great and principal personages are so softened by the Duke's affliction that they are tender of adding to the disturbance of his mind, and therefore most like your friend Ossory will find an easy seat.

I am most truly yʳ affectionate.

LETTER LXXVIII.

April 1767.

MY DEAR JACK,—I have opened your brother's letter to tell you . . . that when the writ was read by the Sheriff at the meeting your Brother made his speech to say he looked upon himself pledgd to the County, . . . but as the gentlemen were inclynd to pay a tribute of regard to their late worthy member (Lord Tavistock) by choosing his relation, he very readily joynd with them in it. . . . Everybody is undone in England,

every day produces new distresses, the immense
expence of the Hunting gentlemen makes horses
and hounds a drug that must be sold, an infatuation runs through the whole plan of living, and
insted of being happy, everyone has made themselves miserable and must all transport themselves
to America.   Lord Chatham is they say, too ill
for bussiness, sees no mortal except Lord Bristol,
sends back unopened all letters from the Ministers,
but yet holds the Helm, which is a most distressing situation for us.   Charles Townshend opend
his Budget yesterday and by a most able speach
adjourned the House for ten days, and sent all
parties home in good humour.   There is, however, all materiel business left undone.   India
Company Affaires is the great object to settle,
and in that Townshend does not draw with Lord
Chatham, therefore he will not see him, nor either
of the Secretarys of State, and nothing conclusive
can pass without his sanction.   For my own part
I conclude he will fling up, and say he cannot
guide.   Bedford has surprized all the House Lords,
for being as composed and seemingly as well as
ever, spoke well and warm.   A charming monody
on poor Tavistock, tis said by Emely who was
his tutor.

Your acquaintance Lord Anglesea is the present town talk.   He was at Lord Lyttletons last
year, and there who made love to his daughter,
who is of a romantick turn, therefore took all his

Oditys for wit, and liked him much. The father did not disapprove, however a month ago he dansed at Almacks with Lady Frances Howard, and made love and proposed to her, after a thousand rediculous things imposible to relate, he went again to Miss Littleton, and then to Lord Carlisle to say he was engaged to Lytleton, but his heart and love was to Lady Frances, this all came to be too serious to persue. Lord Carlisle her brother challengd him, he only answered he had done his family too much injury to add to it and askd pardon. He went to Sir Richard Lyttleton for advice, who told him he ought to go home and be blooded, and never show his face more. Tis said he is gone abroad.

Lord Barrymore who was the whole conversation of last January, is married to Lady Emilia Stanhope, these have been two the most remarkable adventures of this age. Duke Manchester's house is sold to Child the banker for £10,000 guineas.

My dear Jack, Adieu, most affectionately yours.

LETTER LXXIX.

LONDON, *May* 1767.

MY DEAR JACK,—I hope it will be agreeable to you to hurry home as fast as you can, not that there is a certainty of an immediate prospect here, but as the confusion thickens, a convulsion of some sort must be the consequence, . . . therefore hast away and try to find solidity, judgment and sincerity in England, where you will also be sure to find true affection and regard. I conclude the intention of your tour through Italie is to survey the Southern Courts, that you may judge of them in future time, for meerly travelling must be attended with too much expence where there is no foundation for it.

I am afraid you will find everybody sower, there is not a happy face, various causes for it, debt and politicks are chief ones.

Lord Anglesey is married to Miss Lyttleton— a happy pair no doubt.

Our Parliament both Lords and Commons sett late, and many long days there have been lately. Neither India or American Affaires more settled than a month past. The two Irish peers, Barrymare and Anglesea, walk with their Countesses arm in arm at Ranelagh every night. I believe people are rather cautious of being forward in their acquaintance.

We have still fires, and still must call it winter. I hope you will bring summer with you.

Your truly affect.

LETTER LXXX.

CHARLES STREET, 24 July 1767.

MY DEAR JACK,—Your last letter from Pisa left me hopes that a longer time there would establish your health, . . . should any remains of your complaint be still left, our Baths at Bath will be as salutary as those you have left. This day great Thunder and Lightening, I hope it will clear the air, which has been very close and unhealthy some time past. Agues and fevers never known so much in London, everybody in some degree or other from the King, Lord Chatham, to the servants of every house. London is greatly improved since you left it that you will not believe it the same citty. The Pavement is amazing, and the lights in the Squares and Streets so too. If you meet with English papers, you must not depend on anything you read in them, nothing is done, but a great deal doing.

Your truly affect.

LETTER LXXXI.

CHARLES STREET, 8 *September* 1767.

MY DEAR JACK,—I thank you for your letter from Lucca. I am glad you have received benefit from the Baths of Pisa. . . . We have had an irreparable loss in the death of Mr. Charles Townshend, Chancellor of the Exchequer, who dyed last Fryday evening greatly lamented by all people, without dispute the most able, the most knowing, the most eloquent man in the Kingdom, was an acquisition to any Partie that had him, his wit got the preference of his prudence, therefore rather unstedy, but upon the whole he was a most aimable man in all the relations of life, the Publick have a loss, but his Mother and Brother have a much greater never to be repaird, must be sensibly felt by them to their last moments.   A putrid fever has leveled him now with other mortals.   Lord Bute's second son Worteley, who is to enjoy all the Worteley riches, has married himself from the University at Edinburgh to a Miss Cunningham, the Duke of Gordon to a Miss Maxwell, both lucky Scotch ladies.

Poor Doctor Gregory is going, a fever and dropsy, on the declyne, as is your truly affect.

Letter lxxxii.

[The Northampton election spoken of in this letter came off in 1768, and is known by the name of the "Spendthrift Election." Lord Spencer is said to have spent £150,000 on the contest, and Lords Northampton and Halifax £100,000.]

September 29, 1767.

My dear Jack,—Venice is a terible place, very unlucky your fate led you there.   That damp air much more prejudicial than English. . . . Great contests att all elections, and England must be for a twelvemonth to come a most disagreeable place.   Your Uncle, Lord Halifax, was well attended by all his family at Northampton Races. Ld Northampton and Ld Halifax mett there

on extreme good terms, and were to settle the
members for the General Elections. They were
to nominate them at this meeting. Ld Northampton named his brother-in-law, Sir George
Rodney, and Lord Halifax his nephew, Sir
George Osborn, therefore your brother is now in
full employ, feasting and canvassing. . . . For
several years these two families have brought in
by compromise each one member, so there is no
Contest, and the expence a trifle in comparison of
what others are, perhaps four or five thousand
pounds. Sir Robert Barnard says he has £45,000
in his Bankers hands, and will spend it all in
opposition to Hinchingbrook and Carisfort for
Co. Huntington. Duke of Portland engages
against Sir James Lowther. Carlisle, Cumberland, and all the North are in flames by these
potent interests clashing. Lord Edward Bentinck
is sure to come in somewhere, golden showers
water his cause.

Lord Palmerston met Miss Pool at Spa. Those
waters produce many amours, and though ten
years older than himself, is agreeable, sensible,
and so clever, that notwithstanding his intentions
of marrying a fortune, and she has none, yet
Love prevaild, and he was married to her last
week.

Lord and Lady North dind with me the day
before they went out of town, as he would be a
great man soon, I began my solicitations before

he was so, and put in my Claim with regard to you.

Sunday last Wrotesley came express with the death of the Duke of York, there was before that accounts come of his dangerous illness. Perhaps we don't know truth, but they call it a putrid fever, occasioned by his dancing in violent hurrys. . . . I have a terible opinion of all the Physitians abroad, they are absolute Quacks. They are a pert society, and all those abroad are full of the condition of the English, that it is miserable to fall into their hands. Molière well has described them, sets them forth in their true colours, and shews what a state of Body and mind they reduce their friends to.

your affectionate.

LETTER LXXXIII.

CHARLES STREET, 16 *October* 1767.

MY DEAR JACK,—It was your Brother's turn to have wrote now, but the Opposition of Sir James Langham finds him full employment, and he oblidged to scamper away to Northampton this morning. This foolish affair will occasion the two Earls to draw their purses. £800 to each already, a very vexatious circumstance, but your Uncle is determind to go through it at all events, and as they remain 600 a head of Sir James, there seems no doubt it must and will end well.

All this week has been full of surprizes, the Sun has shone most gloriously into this room. . . . George Montagu is appointed Secretary to the Chancellor of Exchequer. Lord North has kissed hands for that . . .

In reading Lord Lyttleton's Harry 2nd, a passage struck me of a letter from good Thobald, old Archbishop of Canterbury, to him, who was the imediate predecessor of Becket. " My flesh is consumd, and my soul is on the point of departing from my body, but it still lingers in hope and desire of your coming, it will not suffer mine eyes to close till they have had the satisfaction of beholding your face," but he dyed before King Harry returned to England, who was then in France.

My dear Jack, most affectionately yours.

LETTER LXXXIV.

LONDON, 27 *October* 1767.

MY DEAR JACK,—The delightfull weather we now have makes me wish you here. . . . The Montreal is not yet arrived with Duke of York's remains, but expected every day. . . . *Nov* 3*rd.* . . . The Contest at Northampton runs high, and the Spenser Interest broke faith severall times. Sir James Langham has, however, given up, used Lord Spenser very ill. . . .

Yesterday morning the Queen gave birth to a

fourth son. The day was strangely devided by joy in the morning and grief in the evening, when the Duke of York's remains were brought from Greenwich, to the Jerusalem Chamber, and are to be interred in Westminster Abbey this evening. I conclude grief has took its seat at your Court, at the unexpected death of the Arch-Duchess Josepha. . . . Never were such stormy contests as now.

yours affectionately.

LETTER LXXXV.

LONDON, 20 November 1767.

MY DEAR JACK,—I am but the shadow of the Grandmother you left in England, and cannot go out of my house, and I find such delay and indolence in everybody that tis very hard and difficult to obtain any Answer. . . . I find the Archduchess is likely to recover the small pox, and conclude she will be your Queen, therefore likely to be with you in the summer, for all preparations for the other will serve for this, the name only changed.

God knows how politicks are to end, at present is quiet, but the Oppositions and money spent by Candidates for the new Parliament has been unknown before. Your brother and Sir George Rodney are oblidged to live at Northampton. . .

Sir George Pocock looks pretty well, he was

M

summoned to Cockpit, Lord Torrington to Duke Grafton's, to hear King's speach, but neither could attend.   Lord Bolingbroke's cause is begun, tis thought her Lord will not be able to procure a divorce.   The town will be very empty this winter, every soul canvassing in the Country.   I shall rejoyce when Parliament is disolvd, and Writs issued for the new one.   Adieu.

LETTER LXXXVI.

Nov. 25, 1767.

MY DEAR JACK,—Your Brother has told you all about Northampton, which principally fills our thoughts . . . there is not the least doubt but he will have success . . . tis infinite the trouble he has, and must for some months have the same. Tis rather stubborn and obstinate in Lord Spencer to set up Lord Howe. . . . Parliament met on Teusday last, all pretty quiet.   Some attempts to amendment of the address, but it soon subsided, one or two flamd away about present mismanagement, but as usual ended in nothing.   The landed Interest is beat out, and Merchants, Nabobs, and those who have gathered riches from the East and West Indies stand the best chance of governing this Country.

Sums unheard off are now given for Cornish Burroughs.   George Byng gives £3000 for one he is oblidged to bring in, and £4000 has since

been offerd for it by another, tho' in honour the
Person must keep to his first purchaser.

LETTER LXXXVII.

CHARLES STREET, *Xmas Day*, 1767.

MY DEAR JACK,—The season, the day, and my
inclinations all press my best wishes to be sent
by my pen. Lord Halifax has received Mr.
Hamilton's letter. . . . I wish you had taken
the resolution in last summer of coming amongst
your friends. North in power, Hillsborough
now Secretary of State to America—two from
whom some good might be produced. . . .

It is found necessary to take in some part of
the Opposition, they have judgd it best to be the
Bedford party, the consequence is—Lord Weymouth, Sec. of State, in room of Conway.

Ld Hilsborough, 3^d Sec. of State for America,
£4000 a year.

Ld Gower, President of the Council.

Ld Sandwich, joynt Post Master, in room of
Hilsborough.

Rigby, joynt Treasurer of Ireland.

Lord Charles Spencer may be one of the
Admiralty if he pleases.

These are the principal changes, only Lord
Gower has kissd hands last Wednesday, the
rest not to do so till after the Holydays.

Duke of Bedford has undergone the operation

of Baron Wesinfield of extracting the Christiline
humour from his eyes—they have been bound up
the proper time after it, and now the bandage is
off he, that was quite blind, sees perfectly well.

Lord Spencer is determind to harass the two
Earls at Northampton, and money without end
will be spent. Ld How's brother has no chance.
. . . Lady Northampton dying has occasiond so
great grief to her Lord that he cannot prevail
himself to go to Castle Ashby. Lord Halifax is
at Horton, your Brother there also, but on Lord
Rothes' death, Duke Gloucester has his regiment,
and all were to be presented to him last Monday.
You never mention Mont Vesuvius no more than
if you were not there.

My dear Jack, wishes of all health and happyness attend you from your truly affect.

LETTER LXXXVIII.

CHARLES STREET, 9 *Feb.* 1768.

MY DEAR JACK,—I freted to be oblidged to
disappoint your expectations of a letter by last
Fryday post. . . . Your brother hurried away to
Northampton. I hope some time next month
we shall be taken out of our boiling water, we
have as yet no fear of loosing the Victory. . . .
March 1. . . . The Parliament now fixd to be
disolvd the 10th of this month. . . . Lord Boling-
brok's divorce is pass, and my Lady is to marry

Beauclerk at once. . . . *April* 12.—Your brother's letter to you Postrestant at Turin will acquaint you of his success at Northampton, tis thought the loosing game to Lord Spencer is at least £50,000, but he will dip farther, and try a vexatious petition to the House. You will hardly credit it when I tell you Wilks is chose for Middlesex, and such a madness reigns, all the town is lighted up on the occasion. . . . So changd is everything since you left us that you have no more notion of our Government, Partie, Conections, than if you were a native of Italy who had hardly ever read of this Country, . . . even the very ladies are changd in dress and behaviour, much, very much for the worse. . . . by my continual attacks you will find me as much changd as all other things. Thank God I am very well resignd to my approaching end, and have no attachment to this world, except your Brother and yourself.

You must forget you come from Palaces at Naples, we will do our best to accomodate you when you return, my dear Jack.

y^r truly affect.

LETTER LXXXIX.

CHARLES STREET, *May* 3rd 1768.

MY DEAR JACK,—Your Brother desires me to writes this post to say he hopes you will not suffer your Servant to bring over anything to sell here, he shall be oblidged to give his word for that. . . .

The Parliament is to meet next Teusday, Lord Spencer enters his petition against your Brother then, the trouble and solicitation is not to be conceivd, ten times more than the Election, the merits of the Cause is certainly with us, but in the House of Commons there is no guarding against Power that transforms numbers and merits into what shape they please. We have most of the leading Interest with us. Ladies enter into this affair, and Lady Spencer obtains all the Belle Esprits to fight their cause as she thinks the men cannot resist them. . . .

LETTER XC.

LONDON, *September* 8, 1768.

MY DEAR JACK,—By the dreadfull accounts of desolation in and about London, which you will read in the newspapers, which are very exactly related, you may wish to have the truth off, I scrible this to acquaint you that you may depend on what you read in them, and therefore I need not repeat, only add that my kitchen and offices below were 3 or 4 feet deep in water. People who keep exact accounts of the weather say more rain fell that day than in the usal course falls in a month, all the land springs have rise to a degree not rememberd by anyone. I received a letter from your Brother today, who says ye Wapineers and seamen are so riotous on the river that a guard has been oblidged to be kept there for the last ten days.   Sure it is a pretty state of things when the lower orders contend against authority !

My best respects wait on Lord Halifax, with the affectionate good wishes of yours,

S. O.

LETTER XCI.

[Bushey was the residence of Lord Halifax.   He died on June 8, 1771, when the peerage became extinct.]

April 30, 1771.

MY DEAR JACK, — Your brother has been at Bushey ever since Sunday with your Uncle.   He will not let him out of his sight.   Inflammation on the Liver.   Dr Thomas carryd down Sir Clifford Wintring Sunday evening, who stay'd all night.

May 3rd.—Your brother's letter will inform you of the dangerous situation your Uncle has been in, indeed, I fear consequences from it. . . . I do not like Jaundice, you know my fear, and calld me a Croaker.   I am very unlucky, however, in my foresights.   Your Uncle let your brother come to town for a few hours yesterday, and says he hopes he may be able to be removed to George Street next Monday if no relapse.   Old age comes on apace with us all, and then what pain and grief is our life.

Your sister has set with me all this last week, as not proper to be out while your Uncle so ill. She sent her excuse to Marlborough House, which she bore very well, but I painted his being a father, and not a common Uncle, and his publick character also demanded a particular decency. . . .

LETTER XCII.

December 18, 1771.

MY DEAR JACK,—I conclude you have met in the newspapers with the extraordinary movement of a bog or morass at Solway beyond Durham of 12 acres which lifted itself up 3 feet and fell again and did so several times, and several days, after which it floted itself off, and coverd all the field, even passed over a river, and covered Land on the other side. Sir Gilbert Eliot and others who are come from Scotland have seen it. None can account for it, only say it is the greatest Phenomenon that has been known.

April 21, 1772.

This Town drest for the Holydays, but dismal in this weather. Good Fryday snowd all day, no comfortable sun yet. . . .

July 25, 1772.

Here is a strange flurry to save the National Bank of Scotland, by a Bank set up at Ayr, Duke

Chicksands Priory 1890

of Buccleugh, Duke Queensberry, and a list of 200 subscribers, . . . and they grant annuitys £800 for 2 lives, . . . all the single ladies are distracted about it, and the topic of all conversation turns on this, but prudent people fear the security, for the Lords and others Estates are most of them entaild, when they dye they cannot bind their heirs, and then what security? The lawyers opinions are all against it, and think it a very great risque, therefore one knows not what to advise any friend to do, so great an advantage bespeaks a snake in the grass somewhere or other, and will turn out a Bank in Air. The Weather has been most exceedingly hot, but Heaven is kind in sending refreshing cooling Showers, and tis thought by coming in this moderate manner that there will be plenty of grain in the field, and fruits in the garden. . . . Only sister Byng and numbers of card-playing widows are in town, that often days pass with me without seeing any mortal. If I could read, write and work as I could till very lately, my time would not hang heavy.

July 6, 1773.

Lord North is now in full fatigue at Oxford, where he is, or will be, chose Chancellor. I think he has passed a disagreeable winter, the papers treat him with great abuse, but I fancy he stands very firm. There is such a want of abilities and such dissipation in living that there is no one to step forth that can succeed to any employment. Lord Chesterfield is come, but I have not yet heard anything with regard to his own affaires, for this town is now too empty to be informed of any thing worth noted. I pass days without seeing any one worth conversing with, so that time passes but heavily, but what can one expect otherways at 80. Swift's Brobdinangs setts that time of life in a miserable light, and can make no one wish to have it prolongd. I am so far happy, that when the release comes, I leave none behind that can want me, and my stay here can only be a clog on those I love.

[This last letter is written after the birth of Sarah's great grandson, afterwards Sir John Osborn.]

17 *July* 1773.

MY DEAR GEORGE,—Next to your brother and yourself this little sensible boy takes a deep hold in my heart, and my prayers are constant that he may be a blessing and comfort to you equal to that you have been to me. I am ever full of a thankful remembrance of God's goodness to me in the most essential point of life, to have been made happy, and very uncommon to be so two generations together. I trust it will extend to the third, in which you may be the partaker of the choicest blessings Heaven can bestow, and that your son will be a worthy member of his family.

Such are the last words penned by Mrs. Osborn.

In Campton Church, Beds., the following inscription is to be seen on her monument :—

The Honb^{le} Mrs. Osborn,
Wife to John Osborn, Esq.,
And only daughter to the Admiral
Lord Viscount Torrington.
Born in Oct. 1693 and died in Novr 1775.
She was a woman
of uncommon abilities and Understanding
Who managed the whole Bussiness
of this Estate
in the two Minorities
of her Son and Grandson,
Sir Danvers and Sir George Osborn.

INDEX.

———o———

MORRISON AND GIBB, PRINTERS, EDINBURGH.

www.ingramcontent.com/pod-product-compliance
Lightning Source LLC
Chambersburg PA
CBHW030550040726
47497CB00008B/2661